Whose Baby Is It, Anyway?
Inside the Indian Heart

This book of essays takes an informal and, I hope, gentle look into South Asian homes, hearts, and homeland in an attempt to help mental health practitioners have a more complete understanding of their Indian clients. My aim is that these stories, anecdotes, and social and psychological sketches may open the door to more pertinent clinical conversations. Just as there is no mother without a child, there is no Indian individual without the family. The focus of western psychotherapy has been on the individual and individuation. My book expands the picture to include the importance of Indian society, family, and culture as an equally, if not more, important path to helping Indian immigrant patients get more clarity from helping professionals. This book can also be of value and interest to the general reader who is interested in South Asian culture and family dynamics.

Whose Baby Is It, Anyway?
Inside the Indian Heart

Kalpana Asok

IPBOOKS.net
International Psychoanalytic Books

International Psychoanalytic Books (IPBooks),
30-27 33rd Street, #3R
Astoria, NY 11102
Online at: www.IPBooks.net

Interior book design by Maureen Cutajar, gopublished.com

ISBN: 978-0-9985323-8-7

To Tom –
without your help, this book would have been
only one half of a conversation.

Table of Contents

CHAPTER ONE

Introduction

I started writing this book primarily for mental health professionals who treat South Asian people. As more of this group reaches out for help from therapists and other mental health providers in the United States, I felt it important for the therapeutic community to be better prepared to serve this population. But as the book began to take on a distinct shape, I realized that this book would be of use and appeal not only to mental health professionals but also to sociologists, anthropologists, and other people interested in the inner life of South Asian people.

Particularly in California, but not only there, there are large communities of South Asian immigrants. People wonder what life is like for people in this community but are naturally shy to ask questions that may seem intrusive or insensitive. There is a general curiosity about the lives of people raised in this other culture, society, and multitude of language(s), but also a particular interest if one works with or has friendships with people whose backgrounds are very different from one's own. Especially in a therapeutic setting, it would be a great disadvantage for the therapist not to know the cultural context of the South Asian patient. I hope to help the reader better understand who the South Asian people are and where they come from, in order to provide a multi-dimensional picture of this unique population.

Who are you? I am making some assumptions about who you, the reader of this book, are. I am assuming you are chiefly a mental health professional who treats South Asian patients or who wants to know more about this group of immigrants. Some of the material can be applied to people from other Asian cultures, as well as immigrants from the Middle East. I am assuming that you know little about the complexity of these cultures, and that you are interested in knowing some background material so that you can become a more effective therapist. As such, my comments are based on what a therapist should keep in mind. I am also aware that some of you may not be therapists, but may be part of the general population who is interested in knowing more about South Asian immigrants. Some of you may be South Asian immigrants yourselves.

Who am I? I am a marriage and family therapist in the San Francisco Bay area, where there is a large population of people from many cultures, including South Asians. I am an immigrant American of South Indian origin, and have lived in the United States for more than twenty-five years. I use the terms *Indian* and *South Asian* interchangeably in my writing, as the majority of my experience has been with Indians, but you can extrapolate this information to the general South Asian population.

I was raised in Bangalore, India, in a Hindu family that was educated and highly privileged. I grew up in a very protected world of love and abundance. I was expected to study, but not necessarily to earn a living—my academic education was an insurance policy against any harsh blows that life might bring my way. I came to the United States, somewhat confused and reluctant, to study and to see if I wanted to be with the person I later married. In spite of this ambiguity, my enlightened parents encouraged me to "go and see what happens." I knew little of external reality—I did not know how to cook, do my laundry, clean the home, or care for myself without servants, the extended family, and the world that I had relied on until then. I had a Bachelor's degree in Biology and Chemistry, had worked for a few years, but had never lived away from my parental home and world.

I have lived the ups and downs of moving away from home, family, and all that is familiar, and have also experienced setting up home, career, and family in the high-energy hectic world of Silicon Valley, California, as many other immigrants from all over the world have done.

It has been a journey that better helps me see and help others like myself.

My immediate family in India lived in a mix of Indian and "other" cultures—part of Indian culture and also on the edge of it. My father's family valued travel and education from the British colonizers, and my father lived and studied in England before returning to India to take on family and responsibilities. My mother's family had strong women who lived very simply, were atheistic (not believing in ritual and religion and therefore part of a very small minority), and strongly believed in higher education for women. My family was *in* it but not completely *of* it. I find myself in a similar situation—living both *in* American culture and Indian culture but not completely *of* either. This is not very different from the sense that a therapist brings to the therapeutic relationship—both of being together and separate—and I will illustrate this to the reader in the chapters to follow.

As I began my journey into the therapeutic world, I heard from colleagues that they might like to consult with me about their Indian clients. I also heard from some of the Indian community that they were more aware of friends' going to therapy and that most of these friends preferred to work with an Indian therapist. The Indian population in the greater San Francisco Bay Area has increased over the last twenty-five years, and that population has settled down in Silicon Valley. Twenty-five years ago, there were about 15,000 people of Indian origin in and around the Valley. As I write this in 2017, we are closer to 110,000. People are raising their children in a different and unfamiliar environment, working hard to balance lives and cultures, rethinking systems they had in place, and incorporating new ways of coping. More Indians are going to therapists for help with family situations that are different and more difficult than the ones they grew up with. The stigma of "needing help" is slowly being replaced by a pragmatic awareness of what help is available.

I am also aware of some South Asians' seeking help from therapists—particularly "American" (read "non-Indian, Caucasian") therapists, as opposed to Indian (read "of Indian origin") therapists. Although there are not too many Indian therapists (this is not viewed as a respected, typically professional career in the way that doctors, engineers and lawyers are), there may be specific reasons for this population to find non-Indian therapists. Perhaps there is a fear of going to an Indian therapist, as s/he may know somebody who knows somebody who knows somebody else in the community, and word may get around. There is a genuine fear of privacy being invaded, as this is still a relatively small population that may not understand the way strict confidentiality works among therapeutic professionals.[1] A therapist raised in India who is culturally and socially aware of the various parts of Indian society makes different sense of terms such as "defense personnel," "central school," "government job," "bank employee," "Jesuit school," or last names like "Iyer," "Menon," or "Khan." These terms and surnames come with a wealth of information about the family that is accessible to anyone who asks for more details about them. A name like "Iyer" has many layers to it—cultural, social, educational, linguistic, religious, math and language skills, etc.—that are difficult to convey. There are ideas that go with these terms that are *Gestalt*—felt experiences where the sum is more than the separate parts. Some of the insights are gained by interactions with people, society and media, not through book learning, but from everyday life experiences.

After overcoming the stigma of needing help from outside the family, many South Asians look for a close cultural fit in a therapist. The reasons for looking for an Indian therapist are variously cited: "they understand us better"; "they know the culture"; "they know what it means when an in-law is coming to visit"; "they have a different experience of family"; "they understand the accent as well as the pressures on the people in the community." When I hear the client's last name and the city he or she is from, I have ideas that usually bear out about which part

---

[1] The Indian population may not be completely informed about the total confidentiality we, as therapists, are held to. It is important to educate our clients about what "confidentiality" means and how it is different from the confidentiality that physicians provide. Perhaps it is also useful for clients to hear that they do not have to tell anyone that they are in therapy, or who is providing the treatment. Additionally, I have found it useful to let my clients know that I will not acknowledge them first if we happen to run into one another outside the office. It would be up to them to greet me or not.

of India the client may be from, what kind of community the family belonged to in India, forming an image—perhaps blurry—of the family's home and social life.

So, who are your Indian clients? When I say "Indian," I am loosely referring to the people who come from Southeast Asia—Pakistan, Bangladesh, India, and Sri Lanka. When I refer to "Indian" customs or culture, I am referring to Hindu customs or culture, as Hindus make up about 80% of the population. When I write about a minority culture like Catholic, Muslim, or Parsee, I will identify it specifically where relevant. I will also explore some unifying themes and values that I see as Indian, as I discuss different aspects of Southeast Asian immigrant life in the United States.

India is more like Europe than America, in that it is a mosaic of color, castes, languages, customs, classes, religions, foods, and art. As of 2017, there are twenty-nine states and seven union territories, and the states are organized along linguistic boundaries. The language of government is Hindi and is the most widely spoken, but each state has at least a couple of official languages. The Indian population is huge—more than 1.25 billion people. About 80% of Indians are Hind<u>u</u> by religion (Hind<u>i</u> is a major language and that of Bollywood), 13% are Muslim, about 2-3% are Christian (usually Catholic), 2% are Sikhs, 0.4% are Jains, 0.8% are Buddhists, and the rest follow Zoroastrianism, Judaism, and Baha'i. About 60-70% of the people follow a vegetarian diet. Food varies with the state, language and subsect. The caste system is still in place, but is less rigid and has less impact in the metropolitan areas of the country. English is understood in most big cities, and those who can afford to send their children to schools where the medium of instruction is English. Most children grow up learning two or more languages and hearing many more.

India won independence from the British in 1947. What had been a loose grouping of princely kingdoms was coalesced by the British into a country—India. After independence in 1947, the Indian empire was split into two countries—India and Pakistan. The Partition was a hugely tumultuous and traumatic time and anywhere from 200,000 to a million people died during the riots and displacement, as more than 14 million people transferred countries and residences, fleeing what had once been their ancestral home and was now a new country with a different religious majority. The newly formed India and Pakistan had many wounds to heal. In 1971, the eastern wing of Pakistan became Bangladesh after the Bangladesh Liberation War. A million people died in the war, and about 10 million became refugees in India. Pakistan is a predominantly Muslim country and a democratic republic with Islam as its state religion. In 1974, Pakistan recognized an independent Bangladesh that is about 90% Muslim Bengali and a multi-party democracy. Ever since Independence, India and Pakistan have been in a low-grade war with sporadic battles as they fight over the muslim majority northern state of Kashmir.

Sri Lanka is also a country that had been colonized by the British and won freedom from it in 1948. It is a diverse country—70% Buddhist, 12% Hindu, 9% Muslim, and 7% Christian (mostly Catholic)—most of whom identify themselves as very religious. 74% of the people are Sinhalese, about 12% are Tamils, and about 9% are Moors. The British brought indentured laborers from India—mostly Tamils, 50% of whom were repatriated to India at Independence, although the first Tamil migration was in the third century. In more recent history, a thirty-year-long violent civil war ended in 2009 and was decided by military force.

Depending on which part of the subcontinent your clients come from, they may have grandparents or parents who remember the Partition or other wars with stories of horrifying atrocities, loss of land and home, and the trauma of having to start life all over again. There may well be multigenerational trauma involving stories of loss and displacement. It is important to take this into account when there is discussion of what effects immigration may have had on the family. In some situations, immigration reawakens some of the trauma that may have been buried or never discussed.

Knowing the when and how of the immigration story and experience of the client gives us a broad category in which to hold the client's experience and background. The recent (in the last twenty to thirty years) South Asian immigrants fall into three large groups.

One group comprises the typical blue-collar immigrants who come to work at jobs in the service sector, like restaurants, driving taxicabs, or running gas stations. They are often from Gujarat or Punjab but may also be from other Indian states. The families of this group are strongly entrepreneurial with an acumen for business. They may be from castes that were traditionally traders, and most likely have a network of people who support each other economically, emotionally, socially, as well as with crucial information. The extended family may be their whole world, providing everything from friendships to finance.

Another large group is the more formally educated group. Often, these people come to the United States to attend graduate school and stay on thereafter to get jobs because they like what they see as the good life. This group is often English-speaking (and probably educated in schools where English was the medium of instruction) and from a more middle-to upper-class background.

A third group is the recent wave of young technology workers, who have come to work at jobs that are equivalent to jobs they would have had in India. Many have gone back to India, and the disparity in incomes is slowly but surely converging, so that many of these workers can have a comparable lifestyle whether they live in India or in the United States. This group is less interested in attending universities here and also less likely to acculturate. They usually have groups of their own, staying very connected to one another in friendship circles that are exclusively Indian. They usually live in areas that have higher concentrations of Indians and, for the most part, like to live as they would in India. Most of them would like to believe that they could pick up and go back to India whenever they decide to do so. As such, they pick and stay within schools and communities where there are strong ties to India, as this is their comfort zone, and also so that they can meld back into Indian communities in India easily.

Something else to consider is whether the Indian family came here directly from India or through another country—for example, Uganda, Kenya, or other parts of Africa. This group may originally have been part of a business community that became refugees, while most in the other groups above made a choice to be here. The therapist should also bear in mind that a person who appears to be a first-generation ("Immigrant+1") Indo-American could have been an immigrant child. Important considerations for this group are how old the child was at the time of immigration, whom they left behind, and how the parents and child coped with missing home and relatives. A grandparent may also have raised this immigrant without the parents for a considerable length of time. I refer to this group as the "I + 0.5 generation."

The reason for migration is an important factor in the first-generation immigrant's life, and clinicians need to be aware of the impact these reasons could have on the mental health of the individual—for example, how is a male who came to the country for graduate study different from a woman who left most of her family behind, coming here to marry a man she has met just once before the wedding ceremony? How does a person who immigrates on a dependent visa, is recently married through an arranged marriage, and who may or may not know his or her spouse well, settle into this culture? Visa status may decide if the person can work outside the home. How are circumstances different for a person who is here on a work permit to take care of a family member's business at a gas pump or restaurant? How is life different for a young girl who has come to study for her undergraduate degree? How does the tech worker manage when she or he may be the sole support of family in India?

Your clients could be from any of the groups above, and their command of English and their level of comfort in this foreign land may differ according to their educational and cultural background. Many of the stories in the book are from interviews. Where I have used actual stories from clients, I obtained their permission and disguised their identities. I am always humbled by the stories brought to me—there are no villains or heroes, just people doing the best they can, making adjustments given the constraints and advantages of personality, family background, immigration, education, and culture, as they try to navigate a foreign culture and world.

CHAPTER TWO

Small Things—The Sacred and the Mundane

In this chapter, I have collected many small insights that add up to something quite large—an accumulation of bits and pieces that, when combined, make up something of Indian culture. Some of these small things are insignificant by themselves, but the quilt they create is of a larger *gestalt*. By *gestalt* I mean a network of habits and psychological, spiritual, and commonly understood gestures in which the whole is greater than the sum of its parts.

Customs, beliefs, and etiquette are vastly different in India compared to the United States. Some of these differences raise questions or create emotional distance between Indians and people who are culturally American. When we know something about a person's background, it is easier to relate to them, and our interpersonal exchanges are richer for knowing it. In looking at Indian customs and culture, it is important not to "exoticize" them or assume that they are somehow uniform across the country. There are many variations in custom and culture within the country, and it is impossible for me to include all the various customs. However, there are aspects of these that I see as common to and important in the experience of most Indians, and I will comment on some of these.

No matter which religion an Indian immigrant follows, or is raised in, the respect accorded to older people is something that defines Indian custom and tradition. It spans informal and formal areas of interaction and is reflected in respectful actions such as standing up when older persons enter the room, not showing them the soles of your feet, getting a drink of water for them, greeting them by asking if they have eaten, and addressing them as "aunty" or "uncle," or appending that honorific to their first names. Older people expect to feel the privilege of their years, and they usually feel loving kindness towards younger Indians who give them even non-verbal indications of being aware of the age difference. Within any group, there is always an awareness of who is older and it is a matter of expected courtesy to help the older person. When an elderly couple was stranded at an airport, the "youngsters" in the group took care of the couple by taking turns getting them food and drink so they could rest instead of walking up and down endless corridors. This kind of group ownership of the elderly is very typical of the way that even Indians who are strangers behave toward other Indians.

Children are expected to give up their chairs for older people, and not expected to need a whole chair for themselves. When seats are in short supply, the children are expected to share or to stand up. When young, children are coddled and made much of, but when they are a little older, they are not always given much room to voice their opinions. For example, teenagers are expected to participate in a conversation when invited to, but are sometimes not invited, and are always expected to know their place in the hierarchy by keeping a respectful silence at certain times and participating appropriately at others.

There is more physical contact with children, and almost all visitors are comfortable interacting with them in a very physical way. Babies get picked up and carried around without explicit parental permission, toddlers get faces squeezed and cheeks gently pinched, and children get their heads patted. In general, there is a degree of comfort with others' children that would be considered unusual in the United States. Children are raised to respect their elders and seek their blessings by sometimes bowing down and touching the elders' feet, shoes, or floor near them with their fingertips, and then ending the gesture with a *Namaste*. In some families, the touching of feet is a daily good-morning ritual; in others, it is reserved for special occasions such as birthdays or other celebrations when blessings are formally sought. It is traditional for young people to go see the elder members of the family on their own birthdays or special days and actively ask for blessings. The older person holds his or her right hand, or both hands, up with palms parallel to the floor, saying, "May you live long," or, "God Bless you," while making small patting motions that signify his or her blessings. Depending on the family and the relationships, touching the feet of elders can be either an expression of love or a substitution for it. Families with elders still living with them, or those who are more traditional, maintain this custom in the United States. In some families, the bowing takes place only in the family *puja* [worship] room, with children also hugging parents to finish the *pranam* or *namaskaram*. In family situations, the clinician may notice that younger people don't challenge or confront older people directly. Sometimes this hierarchy can translate into vulnerable children being unable to protect themselves from older adults in the family. In general, the whole culture is transported to the United States along with the families. The essence of Indian culture is undiminished, even as some ceremonial aspects may be shed along the way.

In some ways, Indians are less verbally communicative in common situations than the average American. There are many levels of nonverbal interaction, including nodding slightly to show understanding or to say thank you. Many Indian people do not use the words "please" and "thank you" as often as Westerners do. These words don't always translate because respect may already be built into the words used in many Indian languages. Indians also reserve these words explicitly for the really important things, and not for every small daily transaction. It is important to be aware that American culture is highly verbally oriented with a great deal of emphasis on "please" and "thank you."

The most common Indian greeting is to say *Namaste*—usually translated as "the divine in me salutes the divine in you"—with palms pressed together and held up to the face or forehead. In business interactions, a western handshake is mostly used, with the understanding that a woman must first offer her hand, and then may choose to nod or select a *Namaste* that involves no touching. This custom is an extension of Indian attitudes that emphasize modesty in clothing—exposure of large amounts of skin is discouraged for both men and women.

There are some other non-verbal gestures to be aware of. It is very important to use your right hand or both hands to offer or receive anything of value. Gesturing at people by crooking your finger and beckoning is considered patronizing and only used in anger towards children or pets. The Indian nod can be puzzling to non-Indians. What looks like a shake of the head can actually be a circular motion of the head, like drawing a horizontal 8 that means "I understand." Most Indians do not like to refuse outright, so people often say "maybe" or "I have to see" and express uncertainty instead. Shoes are usually taken off at the door to people's homes, places of worship, and especially kitchens. An apology is expected if your feet touch another person's, even if accidentally. Kicking is something that brings great disrespect, and people often touch the kicked person and then touch their chest or eyes to show that they are asking pardon and that no disrespect was intended. Some Indian people even apologize like this towards their dog or cat after accidentally tripping on them.

Water is offered to most guests if they turn down a cup of coffee or tea, indicating hospitality and respect between host and guest. The tradition of hospitality stems from a belief that a guest is a manifestation of the divine (it could be a god visiting you) and must be treated with courtesy and an invitation to please come in. In the Indian community in the Bay Area, this tradition of hospitality is still noticeable. When one opens the front door to a neighbor, for example, most Indians would consider it rude not to invite the person in. If the transaction is to take more than a few minutes, it is polite to offer a cup of tea and, if that is refused, to ask if he or she would like some water. This is not just a formality, but also an exchange of pleasantries and an expression of friendliness and hospitality. The formality is extended even to friends who drop by, and the lack of an offer of something to eat or drink is always felt and noticed. A host may say, "You dropped in and chatted—I forgot my manners and didn't ask if you wanted something to drink. How rude of me." The Indian guest may also have noticed it, but will deny it and say something like, "It does not matter, I just ate" to put the host at ease. It is also considered polite to see your guests to the door so they do not have to walk out by themselves, or wait at the door until the guests get in the car or leave the front yard. Indian people notice if the door closes right behind them. And younger people will be considered even more polite if they see older guests out to the car. The general idea is one of a respectful pace of life—people raised in India embrace these ideas, and even if these ideas are not clearly taught to the younger generation, Indians raised in India notice these niceties.

Most Hindu families celebrate at least a few religious occasions a year, also making it a social occasion by inviting people to a meal after the religious aspect of the festival is done. Auspicious times (by the Hindu calendar and according to the planets that influence us) are understood to be important, whether it is newly married couple taking their first trip together, or for the start of an event or project. Most people have an elder in the family whom they would consult for important things in their lives, be it a difficulty that the couple is facing or a financial decision to be made. Most families celebrate the first time a child is fed a meal of solids, usually rice. There is also the ritual offering to the gods of the hair when the child's head is shaved at a temple at about age three that signifies leaving behind unwanted remnants of a previous life as an offering to god. Heads are tonsured for some other reasons, such as a ritual giving up of ego, after the death of a father, or as a penance offering after a vow is made to a god. Children are invited to all events and gatherings, for why would one want to go somewhere without the children? Even if one has no faith in the celebration or no faith in formal worship of a god, there is a secular aspect to most religious celebrations that one can participate in. The celebration is almost a communal one and the physical presence of friends and relatives is highly valued. *Prasadam* [food or flowers blessed by being offered first to a god] are freely shared without asking about one's beliefs, even in a work situation.

Since about the 1960's, the traditional Indian joint family system, where brothers and their families lived close together or in one house, has fragmented with urbanization and modernization. Families in India are still getting used to a newer system, but have lingering guilt and worry about continuing to do the right thing by their aging parents. Men feel they have let their parents down when they are unable to live close to them and support them as they age—even when they live halfway across the world. Some men explicitly talk about taking care of parents and consciously marry women who have brothers so that there is only one set of parents to take care of, the understanding being that one of her brothers would take care of her parents. This is true even when the marriages are self-arranged. Most families spend considerable resources in terms of effort and money for the wedding ceremony, and it is commonly understood to be a time of emotional and social turmoil not just for the couple, but for both of their immediate families. It is most common for the bride's family to arrange and pay for the venue, the meals, the priests, the rituals, and the hospitality for guests of both sides. The dowry system still exists in many parts of the country, and families still incur considerable financial distress when there are more girls to be "married off" with dowries. As women get more parity in education, the system is very slowly eroding, faster in the big cities than in the villages and less developed areas of the country. Many of the freedom fighters of India (and some British officials) tried to educate the masses on women's right to education and to do away with some of the older evils in Indian society, such as child-marriage, dowry, and the lack of rights for widows. Seventy-five years or so after Independence from British rule, it is sad that these changes have not percolated throughout the country. Among Indians in the United States, it is common for both families to share in the wedding expenses, and a matter of pride to some men that they "took nothing" from the "girl's" family, although dowries sometimes are still being asked for in some families in direct and indirect ways.

When viewed from an all-Western perspective, Indian families are very "enmeshed." So, is this good or bad, or somewhere in between? It is good for the family, but may not be so good for the individual. Does the individual really matter that much? This might be a shocking idea for the average American, but it is a very common way of viewing how an individual fits into a family in the Indian system, where the wellbeing of the many comes before that of the one. Duty to the family may have a higher value than the happiness of a person. A common outlook is that you have a responsibility to do your duty and you do not have a right to individual happiness. In return for doing your duty, you may be rewarded either in this life or in the next. If you have a difficult life now, you may be paying for not doing good things in your past life. Your *Dharma* gives you the appropriate *Karma*. This leads to acceptance of life conditions and a stoicism that has a spiritual flavor, but can also be expressed as an unquestioning and passive acceptance of current life conditions. This may lead to a couple's or family's not fighting hard to make changes in their life, but instead being more accepting of unhappiness, even at the cost of more strife and withdrawal from each other. In my opinion, the difference between a parent raised in India who values the family wellbeing over the individual clashes mightily with the child raised in a society that is highly individual-focused. It can be a source of much conflict in a family trying very hard to hold on to their old values, especially if it is not consciously addressed, adding another layer to the usual difficulties that teenagers have with parents.

Western therapists or other interested persons might reassess their concept of what a family looks like, how it fits together, and the importance of an individual's needs and rights. As with many other nontraditional families, Indian families may not fit the mold. Answering some of the following questions with the family may be a good way of clarifying everyone's values and beliefs, and there will probably be differences between the parent generation (raised in India with Indian values) and the younger generation (raised in an American and highly individual-oriented culture.) Do you expect a young person of twenty-five to be living independently, without parents and perhaps with friends? What does it signify if a young man is living with his parents? Is it a practical arrangement? Does the family ever encourage separation? Is it considered part of a natural order? Or, does the family feel sorry for someone who *has* to move away? Is a child allowed to experience any wish to be separate, much less leave the parental home? How does the family hold on to a child? How do they hold on to an adolescent? What are the unsaid expectations of adult children? What are the unvoiced expectations of adult relatives in the area? How does the guilt that an adult child feels (for leaving parents and not physically taking care of them) play out in the family's interactions? And, importantly, how does immigration fit into this picture? Small differences do add up to bigger things; and, often, the smaller choices help people make large decisions, such as which realtor, doctor or decorator to allow into inside spaces and with whom to share more than a cup of *chai*. In my experience, the client is always the family, even if the physical client is an individual.

Many Indian families socialize during the weekends only with other Indian families. Most would be slightly embarrassed by this fact, and many may be also defensive about it, protesting that they do have non-Indian friends. They would all agree, however, that when the group is all-Indian, it is easier to feel completely "at home": that it is unnecessary to explain yourself, or the food, or that the children are running around until late at night, makes for easier entertaining. When they find a group that works well together, they make considerable effort to keep the group going by planning vacations together and birthdays and parties at each other's homes. When the meals are home-cooked, there is a sense of gratitude for the effort put in by the host and hostess, and it is considered an act of humility and graciousness to invest some time in planning. The guests always notice this, and, in such a food-centric culture, it makes a difference. The circle of friends becomes a substitute for the extended family.

In this chapter, I have provided a small introduction to understanding Indian families, their psychology, and the underlying beliefs that make Indian culture what it is. I briefly described behaviors, rituals, and customs that are very important to the Indian community. Some of them are: social hierarchy of elders and of children; non-verbal communication; socializing; taking care of parents; auspicious times as determined by the influence of the planets on our lives; family expectations of individuals, family systems, the rights of the individual as part of the family, and separation from the family systems; and *Karma* and *Dharma*. I address some of these in more detail later in the book.

CHAPTER THREE

A Mother's Words

According to Hindu mythology, and many Indian parents, *Ganesha*, the elephant-headed god of all beginnings, had the right attitude about the importance of parents. *Ganesha* acquired his elephant head after his father, *Shiva*, chopped off his human head when *Ganesha* refused to let *Shiva* enter the chambers of his mother, *Parvati*. (*Shiva* is one of the essential trinity in Hinduism—*Shiva*, the Destroyer, *Vishnu* the Preserver, and *Brahma* the Creator.) *Ganesha* was created entirely by *Parvati* from the sandal paste that she rubbed off her body while *Shiva*, her consort, was away for many years. When *Shiva* returned, he found the way to his wife's home barred by a stranger—a young man who claimed to be *Parvati's* son. *Shiva* then cuts off *Ganesha's* head in an angry rage. When *Shiva* found that *Ganesha* was indeed *Parvati's* child, he was repentant and sent couriers in all four directions to find the head. The only head that could be found was that of an elephant: thus, *Ganesha's* head. *Ganesha*—with his elephant head, special stuffed delicacy in one hand, the broken-off piece of one of his tusks held as a writing instrument in another, and a pot-belly held together by a snake—is considered the god of all new beginnings and is affectionately adored all over India.

Murugan, the younger son of *Shiva* and *Parvati*, was created to slay a demon king who could be vanquished only by *Shiva* or his son. *Shiva* released six sparks from his usually closed third eye and the sparks were carried by *Agni*, the fire-god. But the heat was so intense that *Parvati* took the shape of a body of water to contain it. *Murugan* was the warrior god who emerged from that body of water. He is usually worshipped in his more youthful and boy-like form. *Murugan's* vehicle is a peacock. *Ganesha's* vehicle is a mouse.

Shiva and *Parvati* were given a magical fruit that conferred vast powers. The fruit could not be shared, so they devised a competition for their sons to decide which of them should get the fruit. They asked both boys to race around the world and the winner would get the fruit. *Murugan* on his peacock was confident that he would be faster than *Ganesha* on his mouse. *Ganesha*, however, circumambulated his parents three times instead, saying they were his whole world, and was awarded the magical fruit. This story is often told to children as a moral tale that proves that faster is not better, and that thinking can overrule strength and speed; but the heart of the story is in the point that the parents are the center of the world, and should be a son's whole world.

A son's devotion to his mother is expected to supersede everything else in his life. It is often only after a woman bears a son that she feels a sense of power in her husband's home and family. Until then, she is just the wife. But after the birth of a son, she is the mother of the heir of the house. She fosters his wellbeing with her love, but also with her dependence on him for her position in the home. The mother-son relationship is of such huge significance that it is seen as a son's sacred duty to obey and care for her. A son who does not take care of his mother in her old age feels a huge burden of guilt; and he usually feels the pressure of society and family if he does not do so.

In Indian mythology, a son only ever leaves the parental home when sent on a quest, is banished, or to do penance for a wrong. An adult elder son does not traditionally ever separate physically from his parents, in that he is not expected to set up a separate household. Instead, his new wife moves into his and his parents' home. Although this is changing all over India, along with urbanization, better education for women, and the need for dual-income households that goes with it, cultural biases are slower to change. About four or five years ago, a TV news show targeted at the Indian expatriate community announced that

Vishy Anand, the world chess champion, had won yet another FIDE world title. As the TV announcer smiled and said he had won, she also added something like, "Congratulations to Vishy's parents—they must be very proud." It did not matter that he was then a grown adult, or, that he had a wife and children.

The death of the patriarch in many Hindu Undivided Families leads to battles for succession, especially because many Hindus believe it is bad luck to write a will. In a well-known incident concerning a family known for their industrial leadership and wealth, a rift broke out between the sons that was compared to the infamous rivalry of the cousins in the Hindu myth *The Mahabharata*. The brothers fought for control, all the while avoiding a direct face-to-face confrontation—with the younger brother responding in culturally respectful terms, such as appending *bhai* [brother] when referring to his older brother. When the battle went to the High Court of India, the brothers were advised to go back to their mother and seek her help in brokering a truce. Although the brilliant and ambitious father had created the company, the mother was seen as crucial to their business empire and to the recreation of harmony between the brothers. Throughout the years the case was in court, the brothers and their families lived in the same building and supposedly still shared food made in the common family kitchen under their mother's supervision.

Cricket is a madness, a passion, a tremendous force, and the game that can hold the entire Indian subcontinent in thrall. Sachin Tendulkar is one of its megastars, a super-power in his own right, and possibly the best batsman the game has produced. He is mobbed wherever he goes and the crowds adore him. Most important, people appreciate his modesty, his values of hard work, his dedication, and his devotion to his family. When he announced his retirement in 2010, his mother finally came to watch him play. Until then, she said she was so anxious about how he would perform that she could not bear to watch the match, even on TV. When the crowds were going wild and there were standing ovations, he ran up to his mother and asked her if she had brought him sweets, as she usually did after every game. It was reported that the entire stadium stood up for her when she entered it. Shortly afterward, when Sachin was awarded the *Bharat Ratna*, India's highest civilian award, he dedicated it to his mother and then to all the mothers in India who sacrifice so much for their children's prosperity. It is not enough that he is a good husband to his wife and father to his children. It is that mother comes first, and this is certainly a quality that is as much touted in Bollywood as it is in real life. Sachin is not just a great sportsman, but also a good Indian male role model. His dutiful and loving relationship with his mother makes him a superior role model in India.

Telephone companies with calling plans to India have TV and print ads that show an essential part of family life—children calling their parents. The scene displays images of three generations talking—grandparents, adult children, and their children— usually on a weekend morning, everyone relaxing at home, with the children taking turns talking to grandmother and grandfather, who are beaming. Everyone is expected to talk to everyone else: to exchange greetings and ask if traditional foods were made or eaten, if firecrackers were set off for *Deepavali* [Hindu festival of lights in October or November], if new clothes were bought for these occasions, and if children are studying and eating well. The India call is an expected part of the weekend for all in the family, and newlyweds in particular, take this seriously as they set up new relationships and traditions.

It is considered really important to get the blessings of the elders in the family and great store is set by these blessings. When there is no "elder" in the family because the older parents have died, it is very common for young and even middle-aged people to informally adopt aunts or friends and actually say to them that they are now the elders for the family. The family will then imbue these persons with respect and affection, visiting them for holidays, inviting them for meals, and formally bowing to them and touching their feet to ask for blessings. To not have an elder in the family constellation is to feel afloat and unanchored in the world, causing distress to the adult members of the family. When the mother-in-law and daughter-in-law do not talk to each other, there can be stress felt throughout the family, giving rise to considerable tension between the husband and wife. If the daughter-in-law and the mother-in-law do not get along, the friction between them extends further than just the two of them. The whole family feels the impact of the loss of harmony, and the son feels considerable stress being caught in the middle.

General media (like TV, movies, and news sources) in the United States communicate some cultural beliefs, values, and expectations that are part and parcel of life in the West. For example, it is almost expected that when a young man leaves for college at the age of eighteen, he will call home when he needs something, and that he will get absorbed in friends and fun and life among young people like him. It has almost become a parody of a Western college-age child that he or she only calls parents when money is needed. Most Indian families expect their sons to call or communicate with parents at least once a week. Relatives ask about the calls and their frequency, and feel that all is good if there is consistent weekly communication. Families will proudly say to their friends that they have a good son, and that he calls his mother (more significant than calling his father) every week.

Daughters are expected to call even more often than sons, and are charged with the idea that the primacy of this relationship is of the utmost and that mothers are good resources. In most Indian families, the mother-daughter bond is expected to be strong and vibrant, with the daughter loving, respectful, and caring towards her mother. In a group of American women, if one of them announces that her mother is coming for a visit, there are various facial and other reactions from the other women in the group. They express surprise (if it is not a holiday seasonal visit), raised eyebrows that say "Why now?," expressions of concern as in "Is everything OK?," or a cautious and tongue-in-cheek "Have fun." There is implicit understanding that a mother needs a reason to visit. In a group of Indian women, the reactions would be very different, even if it were a visit within India and not a visit to the United States. There would be expressions of "How lucky," envy (you get to relax and be taken care of), and smiles of contentment. And the women would comment about the one whose mother is visiting by saying things like, "Look at her, so happy, you can see she is enjoying mother's food!" Indian girls are not expected to struggle so hard to individuate and separate from their mothers, although there are the usual teenage tantrums and pouts. More importantly, a woman's girlfriends would not do the American equivalent of the "eye roll" or make other "dissing" non-verbal expressions that signify a joint understanding of "Oh, mothers are so frustrating." It is more common that a person assumes a good relationship between a girl and her mother, even during the difficult teenage years. Larger groups in society also look upon the relationship with joy. The idea of what should be expressed takes precedence over the actual realities of a particular family's connections with the mother.

The idea of a mother's words and their importance is conveyed by the story of how the *Pandavas* cared for their mother. The five *Pandava* princes and the story of their battles and skirmishes with their cousins the *Kauravas* make up *The Mahabharata,* one of the great Indian epics. (The *Bhagavad Gita,* or the *Song of God,* is the "Bible" of Hinduism in which the God *Krishna* tells the *Pandava* Prince *Arjuna* to do his duty without being attached to the fruit of the actions, even if it involves killing his cousins.) The *Pandava* princes took their mother's words seriously when one of them—*Arjuna*—won the hand of a princess in a contest that involved archery skills. The mother, without looking to see what it was that her son had won, told him to share equally with his brothers, and thus the five princes shared one wife. This is a story of extreme obedience of sons to their mothers that is upheld as a virtue to most Indian children.

When young couples meet through non-traditional ways, most of them will wait for their parents to consent to the match, and rarely marry without some signal of acceptance by the parents, especially the mother. It is not uncommon for them to wait as long as a year, given the importance of obtaining parental blessings and acceptance. There is always the underlying assumption of needing to have harmony in living together as a larger family, even if not under the same roof. Young girls are raised with implicit values of not breaking up the family. An Indian girl's fantasy of a future husband almost always includes a mother-in-law figure who will be helpful, kind, and another mother to her. The reality is that there is often conflict with the mother-in-law, at least in the first few years, as they work out a balance in the relationship. The presence of a mother figure in the future family is always part of the marital landscape. When exploring an arranged marriage, the personality of the mother-in-law is a key factor in making the decision. The girl marrying into a family gets absorbed into that new family and her everyday life may be impacted more by her in-laws than her husband. In traditional families, the daughter-in-law stays at home and may spend more time with her in-laws than with her husband.

Anita, a neighbor's daughter, was in love with a young man she met at her workplace and they soon intended to marry. When she met her fiancé's family, things changed for her. She began to see that her parents, with whom she had a cordial relationship, would have a difficult time with her fiancé's family. She found that her future mother-in-law was condescending to her well-educated parents, was "money-minded," mean-spirited, and spoke ill of her own daughter. Moreover, her fiancé did not speak up for his sister and she felt uncomfortable marrying the entire family. As the only child in her family, she was certain that her broad-minded and generous parents did not deserve this family relationship, so she broke it off with her fiancé. She found him attractive, but that was not enough to overcome her qualms about her future mother-in-law—he also had to be strong enough to manage his parents, who would be an integral part of the whole family unit. She began to see a lot of trouble ahead for herself if she were to marry him.

Even though I discuss mothers more than fathers in this chapter, I want to emphasize the extreme importance of filial duty to both parents and the enormity of this relationship in Indian families. Men feel immense guilt when they do not take care of their parents, especially their mothers, in the expected ways.

For example, Rahul, a young man I met with, believed he would die of emotional overload if he were to go back and see his parents, whom he had turned his back on because of conflicts between his wife and his parents. He lived with such a heavy burden of guilt that he became sure he would not survive meeting them again. He could not bear the shame of meeting them and looking them in the face, because he had failed them in the most crucial duty. Needless to say, his marriage eventually became an empty husk. He did his duty to his children, but his anger at his wife for her part in not accepting his parents converted into a cold fury—he stopped eating anything she cooked. Not eating food that is cooked at home carries huge symbolic and specific meaning, especially in Indian culture.

A second example—in another family, the couple resolved their differences after the man, Ram, had an affair, but it took considerably longer for him to patch things up with his disappointed and shamed parents. Until this was done, the reconciliation was not complete. The need for parental approval transcends distance, time, and age, but the guilt an Indian man feels for abandoning his parents is extreme.

Mother's Day and Father's Day are not celebrated formally in India, but the Western concept is slowly gaining ground in the last decade as commercialization and card-and gift-giving traditions from the United States are carried into Indian culture. Commonly, those Indian parents who send their children to the United States adopt some American holidays in the exchange of culture that goes along with children's moving between two worlds. Hinduism designates days to celebrate and acknowledge siblings, spouses, and ancestors, but not living parents. As many Indians joke, every day is Mother's Day for those of us lucky enough to be Indian! A parent's sixtieth birthday and eightieth birthday are celebrated by re-performing the couple's wedding vows, an event that is usually conducted by the grown children. Most Indians who are able to afford it talk to their parents at least weekly, and look down upon yearly celebrations to honor their parents.

It is, of course, essential to a man's self-regard and pride that he support his parents financially when needed. He is viewed as a failure among his peers in the Indian community if he does not support them as they age. When a couple has disagreements about the use of their money, and the man is not able to send money home to his parents, he feels much less of a man and feels intense shame as well as anger towards his wife if the pressure not to send money home has come from her. In turn, she is also viewed as selfish, uncharitable, and an unnatural daughter (in-law). In more recent years, parents who educate their daughters as well as they have their sons in the past do expect their daughters to care for them financially. Even as the world of education and industrialization change in India, some things such as "social security" for parents stay the same. Parents put more into their children and their education without saving for their own retirement, based on the social and cultural assumption that their children will, of course, take care of them as they age. When parents live a simpler and more humble life, but struggle to educate or support their children so they move up in the social and economic ladder, the parents expect financial support in return. When the parents have enough that they do not need financial support from their children, they still expect emotional and psychological support in the form of phone calls, visits, and the physical closeness of living near-by or even with them.

A friend belonged to a book club that had Indian and American women. One of the American women was not close to her mother, who lived by herself in a different city. When the members heard that her mother had died alone, they were all sorry for her loss. The Indian women, however, were more than sorry. They were angry with their friend, and mostly horrified that she could have permitted this to happen. They all but accused her of neglect, because they found it so intensely appalling that she had not even been in regular phone contact with her mother. When a mother is in her eighties or older, Indian people expect that the person will not want to be alone, and expect that a good daughter or son will provide help for her, calling and checking on her wellbeing every day. In the book group, the Indian women were very troubled by how the American woman dealt with her mother's death in such a calm and detached manner. The American women, on the other hand, found the Indian women to be judgmental and could not understand the uniformity of reaction of all the Indian women.

"All alone" is regarded with horror and is the worst kind of death, even though we all do die alone in some sense. A couple living in the United States will feel "all alone" during festive occasions—not just missing family and home, but truly feel alone in being without the whole family nearby. In fact, it is common to hear a couple say, "we are all alone here," paying no attention to the word "we" in their comment.

A mother becomes almost the more real of the two parents, and she symbolizes the "mother of childhood." Children will do almost anything to please her, and become desolate if they cannot please her. All power resides in her and to not take care of her is to not honor life and duty, and is simply bad *dharma* and therefore bad *karma*. Devotion to mother is not just to the actual mother, but also to the metaphoric sacred mother, and is an essential principle of Indian culture.

CHAPTER FOUR

Spirituality and Religiosity in the Home

oshni called me, asking for psychotherapy to get help with her oldest child. He was twenty-one and about to leave home for the first time to start a job in another state. A lot had happened in the family and Roshni decided they could all do with some help. "My son has a good job, but he has decided he will not go to the East Coast anymore" was her first sentence on the phone. When she came in to see me, I heard the rest of the story, which really should have been the start of the story.

About a year ago, her husband Sayid had been diagnosed with cancer and had begun treatment. He had been making good progress and the whole family was relieved when the cancer went into remission. Sayid and Roshni come from a devout Muslim family in India. Their extended and immediate family in India said all the customary prayers on Sayid's behalf, and performed ceremonies in keeping with their beliefs. It had been a difficult year for the whole family, but, according to Roshni, they had navigated it safely.

More recently, in the last month, her husband had begun to behave strangely. He hid the valuables in the home, closed down several bank accounts, and packed his bags. He verbally divorced Roshni, saying "*Talaq, Talaq, Talaq*" in a calm detached voice. *Talaq* is commonly understood in the Muslim culture in India to be a word with final symbolic significance. In Islamic culture in India, a triple talaq is an authoritarian, legal, and binding, but accepted, way for a person to initiate and complete a divorce without any court involvement. Roshni insisted that she and her husband were close—good friends above all—and that this was not the husband she knew.

According to Roshni, her husband's oncologist was "too American" and was encouraging Sayid to "find his bliss." She wanted to be sure that I understood Indian and Islamic cultures, and would not "encourage unusual behavior," that I would not provoke the family to break up without a really good reason. Her first visit to me was by herself.

When I met the couple during the next session, they both seemed relaxed and there was no mention of divorce. Roshni said that both sides of their families had suggested that a priest come home and bless them. The priest, who has known the family for over ten years, came to the house, blessed the couple and the family, and announced that there had been evil forces and that someone had done "jadoo" to the family. "Jadoo" translates to magic, but what the priest meant was that someone had cast an evil eye on the family. He proceeded to perform certain rituals to counteract those forces, and Sayid nodded as Roshni said that everyone was feeling better after the priest's visit and cleansing rituals.

Somewhat Westernized, Roshni and Sayid are both elegant and well-dressed, come from families that are educated, and carry themselves with the easy confidence of people of considerable wealth. Sayid works in "finance, mergers and acquisitions," and Roshni is a homemaker who is busy taking care of extended family, children, and the homes they own.

Sayid's father died when he was a little boy. His mother and all her brothers and sisters raised Sayid. After his sisters married, he looked for a suitable match for a long time and found in Roshni "the woman of my dreams." It also was important to him that he marry someone whose "whole family was alive." He spoke emotionally about how close he is to Roshni's family as well as to his extended family. He was very frank as he admitted that his will to survive and beat the cancer arose from his desire to make sure his son was still going to have a father. When asked about what else happened in the family, Sayid talks about his father-in-law. About six months ago, his father-in-law had a stroke, and, although he is recovering well from it, Sayid admits that it was soon after the stroke that his own will to live and beat the cancer wavered. He talks freely about his admiration for his father-in-law, his attachment to him, and his views about him as the role model he did not have in his childhood. He has, however, not consciously considered what the possible death of his father-in-law would do to him.

When his oncologist encouraged him to "live his life," Sayid saw a chance to leave all his responsibility and try to be different. He smiles at his wife as he says, "Sorry, I was so clumsy and muffed it all up." Roshni's body visibly relaxes. Sayid then looks at me and says, "I have to do some different kind of work now, don't I? My son will be okay now."

The role and importance of the priest is equal to that of the extended family as he encourages the man in the family once more to take on—even in the face of illness—the role of protector. The priest carried out rituals with the family, ridding the home of intrusions and bringing the couple back together with sacred rites. The priest characterizes the intrusions as the "evil eye."

In my view, the intrusions are many. The cancer certainly is the primary one. The stroke, threatening the loss of an important father figure, is another. The forthcoming separation from his son is a pending loss. The unsuitable freedom proposed by the "too American" oncologist is a different kind of intrusion that Sayid has not been able to combat culturally. Roshni was wise in bringing in the priest, as "advised by my mother-in-law," and in adding me to the mix. It was unthinkable for Sayid to break his family apart, and not in keeping with his personality. His warmth and sense of himself are not things apart from his family, but an integral part of it.

The above story illustrates the power of religious ceremony in an Islamic family, and its significance and position in the households of South Asians. Larger Hindu homes have a small room dedicated to prayer and rituals. One of the adults, usually the primary married mother figure, has the privilege of lighting the oil lamp every morning after a shower. Children are taught and encouraged to build a moment of prayer into their morning routine, even if it is only two seconds of bowing their heads with hands folded in *Namaste*, prostrating on the floor in front of the *Puja* [prayer] room. In more modest homes, at least a shelf in the kitchen is set aside for a lamp and a couple of images of gods and goddesses. On Fridays and special feast days, a dessert or other special food offering is put in front of the gods. Then prayers are said over it, and the *Prasad* [blessed food] is distributed to the family. This is the everyday routine in the majority of Hindu households.

In India—even in scientific institutions of higher learning and research—Hindu religious belief comes into play. Every year, during the *Navrathri* celebration around September [nine nights of festivities dedicated to the goddesses signifying the triumph of good over evil, and light over darkness], there is one night and day dedicated to the Goddess of Learning, *Saraswati*. People venerate the objects in their lives—books, tools, cars, musical instruments, anything that impacts their learning and life. Research centers and their computers, telescopes, spectrographs, radiation equipment, medical equipment, X-ray machines, lathes—everything comes to a halt. During this holiday all over the country—although essential services everywhere do not come to a complete halt—many services do stop for the day, or at least an hour or so is dedicated to revering the objects that represent learning. Objects are placed in the *puja* room, or are garlanded with flowers, incense is lit in front of them, and they are given a symbolic day of rest. Cars and buses drive around with garlands hanging off their bumpers, offerings are made to the Goddess, and children are usually delighted to have a day off from study. This day supposedly unites all religions in India, and almost everyone participates in some way to observe the day. But, of course, it could be that the Hindu majority overwhelms the whole country.

When there is a special event, such as a birthday, Indians offer special prayers to the gods in a temple. This is in addition to the prayers at home in the name of the person whose birthday is observed. And they make a favorite dessert as well. Cakes are a newer and western addition to the traditional customs, probably brought in with the British invasion.

If there is a series of illnesses, accidents, or difficulties (social, psychological, academic, or marital), one of the first steps in securing the home and family is to consult an elder—an aunt or uncle or grandparent who will invariably include a religious ceremony or a special puja as part of the attempt to bring things back in balance. The goal of the puja is to bring peace and harmony, as well as a feeling of togetherness to the family, which emotionally equips them to face the challenges ahead. In addition, the family may consult astrologers, seek out doctors, and hire tutors to address the issues being faced. As families have modernized, and moved away from the joint family system, some of these traditions have been retained and others lost. Uncles and aunts may not understand the pressures faced by families who live in a different country. They may also not have experience living in cultures where outside help is expensive, and where both members of the couple work outside the home. The generation of young couples who are in their twenties and thirties worry less about the stigma of psychotherapy and are more willing to get counseling from a professional therapist. For those clients who are culturally very Indian, the importance of a therapist who can understand the inside of the home is crucial to their accepting therapeutic words into their inner space. Otherwise, the therapist remains an outsider.

Many families that were traditionally vegetarian as part of religious practice have switched to eating meat. Some of these families are completely comfortable with the transition. But, for many others, the family members may eat non-vegetarian foods outside the home and in restaurants, but will not actually cook these items in their kitchens inside the home. Most Hindus will still avoid beef, as the cow is considered a sacred animal that produces life-sustaining milk. The home is to be separate and sacred, and is to be sheltered from such unaccepted practices that violate tradition. Some families in which part of the family eats non-vegetarian food may even have a separate outdoor kitchen and dedicated pots and pans to cook with, so that the meat cooked does not pollute the rest of the home.

Having a dedicated space in the center of the home for *puja* and lighting a lamp is symbolic of the understanding that the home and family are part of the divine, and that the home is a holy sacred space where there should be peace. Each person may have a favorite deity or god—a personal relationship with God is at the heart of Hinduism. Lighting a lamp is a daily attempt to recapture ritual, peace, and contentment. It is a meditation of a few seconds and an act of intentionality signifying hope and commitment to spirituality in the home.

CHAPTER FIVE

New Clothes Over Old

Love is on the rise. I have learned—anecdotally, socially, and through interviews with people of Indian origin in this country—that over the last fifteen to twenty years the number of "love marriages" has increased in the Indian community in the United States. This is a reflection of the same phenomenon's occurrence in India. This change in how people choose spouses has not been accompanied by an emotional move away from parents, as usually happens in Western cultures. The young couple and the parents of the couple expect that the family function will be the same as in any traditionally arranged marriage. The parents accept the new member of the family either with or without a struggle. The young couple accepts the new family members in the same manner as they would have had it been an arranged marriage. Things like the respect, the courtesies, the ways of speech, and the exchange of greetings on important dates all stay the same. Most important, the symbolic positions of the parents-in-law do not change just because the marriage was not arranged. It is almost as if the whole family system ignores the fact that the marriage was not arranged, and things go on just as before. In fact, as soon as the parents come into the picture, or are invited to meet each other, the old ways take over and the hapless couple is carried off on the old-time traditional tides. The whole family system does not know how to do this new thing, so it reverts to the old comforting ways.

For example, who should make all the arrangements for the wedding event? It used to be traditional that the bride's family took care of the logistics and work of the wedding itself. The groom's family came to the event, was waited on, pleased, pampered, and mollified if they expressed unhappiness with any of the arrangements. (The groom's parents and family wield outsize power and they are feared in many Indian communities. There are thousands of incidents of the ceremony being disrupted by demanding parents asking for more and better, embarrassing the bride's family, and sometimes ruining their son's relationship in the name of pride and status.) If the couple is in conflict about these arrangements, they do not have a new way to resolve this. In short, a "love marriage" does not automatically imply change in other traditions. Sometimes couples find themselves in conflict over this unexpressed implication. One half of the couple may have understood that the "love marriage" meant that there would be discussion and concordance between the couple, and therefore between the in-laws, on most family events. By "arranged," I mean that parents, relatives, friends, interested middle parties, or newspaper advertisements helped the families find each other. Then the families met, made inquiries in the vast network of relatives and friends, and—together with the bride and groom, astrologers, and priests—arranged the marriage and the terms of the actual wedding ceremony. In these arrangements, a great deal of attention is paid to the caste, community, and sub-caste of the families, as well as to the people, so that the differences between the two families are very small. This process ensures that the bride and groom typically end up being from similar social, religious, cultural, and financial backgrounds, with clear expectations of their roles and relationship to each other and to the families.

In arranged marriages, the expectations of each other and the respective families vary according to the community and their cultures. It usually follows an expected path—in the first few years, there is more sweetness between the couple as they get to know each other, but dust-ups are also expected as the families negotiate back and forth, coming to terms that are socially expected and normative. Most couples expect that there will be misunderstandings that will eventually be resolved. In the typical arranged marriage, happiness and compatibility between the couple is not the sole expected result, but a fortuitous outcome that may happen as a side effect. The stability of the entire system is the primary goal, rather than the happiness of individuals in the marriage.

Indira and Jay came from well-established trading families in a South Indian city. When Indira left her maternal home to go and live with Jay's family in the same town, there was a certain amount of tension felt by all. How were the families going to manage the proximity? Was Indira going to be at her maternal home on many visits or "there all the time?" How were they going to prevent too much familiarity between the in-laws' families? How would she transition to her married home if she went back to her parents' home every other day? Would she be at her maternal home so much that she would not become part of Jay's family? Although Jay did not mind if his wife was away every day for a few hours, he began to pick up the hints thrown by his family that he should "control" Indira and not let her leave everyday.

So this situation would be one that everyone could see, understand, and expect. It was also expected that Indira would do things to ensure smoothness in the transition—she would aim to please her in-laws, she would improve the home through furnishings or adding furniture, she would maintain and increase contact with Jay's siblings and cousins and add them to her set of friends, and she would in general try to smooth rough patches of misunderstandings between the two families. These kind of difficulties are expected, openly talked about, and part of the drama of the first few years of an arranged marriage.

In the great transition from a system of parent-arranged marriages to "love" marriages, there are some significant stops along the way. There is the semi-arranged marriage, the e-dating marriage, the dating-for-some-time and then handing-over-decision-to-the-parents marriage, and the dating-then-love marriage. The importance of the parents in the wedding planning and arranging, the reluctance to do away with a system that has worked for the most part, and the importance of the parents' role after the wedding are all affected in different degrees by the "new" kinds of meeting and marrying.

Suja is a recent medical graduate who is in the process of finishing her residency in a local hospital. She is about 27 years old, has good social skills, is pleasant looking, soft-spoken, and speaks with an American accent. She was born and raised in the United States. She has tried to date Indian men who are "*ABCDs*[2] like me" and who are immigrants like her parents. She says that she is tired of relationships that go nowhere quickly, but does not seem to know why or how they go wrong.

Suja is considering a career in pediatric surgery. As she finishes her residency, she is living with her parents and then plans to move close to wherever she gets a job. She is noticing that several of her friends are either seriously dating or close to getting married and worries about her "lack of dating luck." At first, Suja's parents tried the traditional method to help her find a partner, by speaking to relatives in India and the U.S. and passing her horoscope around. The reliance on horoscopes is more prevalent in South Indian families. The very traditional families would consult their own family astrologers, who would compare the two horoscopes and then flag the pair as compatible or incompatible. The astrologers would take into account personalities, family compatibility, stressful times in the two lives, and other factors by the presence of the stars and planets in different "houses" of the horoscope at the time and location of their birth. When both astrologers had agreed on compatibility, the parents talked to each other and then set up a time for the families and the couple to meet.

Although there were four such horoscope-compatible matches for Suja, her parents did not like two of the families they met, which prevented Suja from meeting the two men or "boys" in these families. In the third family match, Suja talked to the boy, liked him, and met him one more time at a café—outside of the family meeting and on her own. During this meeting, he told her that he was actively dating a gori or "white girl" whom his parents did not know about. He said he liked Suja, and wished he could make himself and his parents happy, but was unable to break up with his girlfriend. So, Suja and he told their respective parents that they were not suited to each other.

Fifty years ago, in a family like Suja's, there would have been just one

---

[2] ABCD stands for "American-Born Confused Desi." See Chapter Nine for more information on this designation.

family meeting and the marriage would have proceeded. There are still many families who would put a lot of pressure on their children in such a situation, pressing and arguing for this match. If Suja and this boy had both said "yes" to this match, this would have been a semi-arranged match. "Semi" because the couple would have had an opportunity to go out and get to know one another for a while before they got married. In the fourth horoscope-matched family, Suja found the boy unattractive, passive, and did not like the way he spoke or dressed. So, she herself decided he would not do for her. Suja then embarked on e-dating, signing herself up on several Indian matchmaking sites.

She had mixed luck on them. At first she was flooded with many names and learned to weed out those who were interested in her as a stable breadwinner and/or ticket to a green card or permanent residency visa status. She corresponded with a few she thought suitable—they spoke the same language at home and were educated like her. A couple of these men wanted to talk about sexual compatibility, and proposed weekends together. Suja found herself unwilling to go away on these weekends. She wanted a deeper relationship first—on the phone, via email or chat, and then meeting for dinners. These matches seemed to not really include dating in the traditional sense. She began to narrow her search to her city and state.

At this time, she began to understand her lack of dating skills. During middle and high school, she was not allowed to go to the school dances and mixers. Her parents thought that these events did not accord with their cultural values, and she did not fight to go to them. She also was so busy with scheduled after-school activities and studies that she had no unstructured time to "hang out" with friends. In college, she went out in larger groups of friends to events and dinners, but refused dating invitations from non-Indian men, even when she liked some of them. She was friendly with three or four girls, but seldom invited them home or went to their homes. She said her parents were not unfriendly, but they were socially awkward with non-Indian people, and she was ashamed to say she was actually embarrassed by them. Now, as an almost newly fledged doctor, she had little to no experience dating.

Suja started dating earnest young Indian techie men similar to herself in their lack of dating experience. She had more in common with this group of new immigrants. Her most recent date is a man she respects for his values, his simple lifestyle, his affectionate relationship with his parents and sister, and his naïve innocence. But, she says, "I wonder if he is gay?" Although there is an emerging population that is open about their sexual identity and dealing with parental anger, disappointment, and perhaps acceptance, she also is well aware of the many Indian men and women who deny their own homosexual identity. Some of these men and women get married to keep their parents happy and lead double lives. If Suja continues to date this young man, she would most likely choose the "dating and handing over to the parents" style of marriage. There is a real pull to go back home to a more comfortable style of managing the plans for the wedding. Responsibilities are handed back to the parents at this stage, and their blessings imply that they take ownership of the relationship from then on, including interacting closely with the groom's parents.

In some situations where couples meet through e-dating, the two are more likely to hand the package back over to their parents if they come from more Indian and less westernized families. In situations where the parents are culturally more westernized (in their habits, values and homes), with more exposure to non-Indian friends and lifestyles, the couple takes on more ownership of their life together, including the planning of their wedding and an accompanying emotional move away from their respective parents.

Kittu and Lakshmi met through an online dating site for Indians. They belonged to the same caste and community, spoke the same language, and felt comfortable with their shared tastes in music and movies. They were both getting master's degrees in universities in the USA. They "dated" electronically for a few months, met each other over a weekend at Kittu's college town, and then, after a lot of talking on the phone for a few more months, decided to get married. They each told their parents that they had found someone they wanted to marry. This kind of dating does not really match the Western concept of dating, and it does not match the Indian concept of an arranged marriage either. It is somewhere in the middle.

As soon as Lakshmi and Kittu got the parents involved, the old procedures automatically took over. Lakshmi's parents had to please Kittu's parents, the grandmothers from both sides had to be respectfully addressed, in-laws had to be invited to religious functions with the proper decorum and formalities followed, and both parties retreated to their zones of comfort. The parents probably even asked each other if their homes were owned or rented, and to whom properties owned would be bequeathed. The families would make sure their children would be treated fairly regarding inheritances. For example, if Kittu had a sister, there might be discussions about who would inherit the parental home.

The wedding planning became an event in which there was almost no acknowledgment of the bride and groom's choosing each other. It does not automatically follow that if this is a marriage of self-choice, there could be room to do things differently according to the wishes of the bride and groom. In fact, these may be the wishes of the bride and groom. Everyone got swept up in the preparations. According to Lakshmi and Kittu, there was no going back after this stage. If they expressed the slightest doubt or hesitation about each other, the families got together and told them, "It will all be fine, why worry?" Everything functioned as if it were a regular arranged marriage. According to Kittu, who is a little more modern in his thinking, "They even wanted me to formally propose to her in front of the whole family." He found it strange, but no one else did—it was after all, a family thing.

There are aspects to this kind of relationship that are also somewhere in the middle. The couple have expectations of each other that are formally romantic: they want each other to plan their birthday parties; they like to and expect to receive gifts from each other; they expect to be treated as if they love each other; and there is considerable pain expressed when these expectations fall below the norm. The dust-ups that are expected in the traditional arranged marriage are not so well tolerated in these quasi-romantic matches. It is almost as if the couple magically expect that this marriage should follow another path—of romance and the traditional, side by side, both old and new.

If there is a lack of compatibility, sexual and otherwise, that is discovered after a few years of marriage, it is possible that the couple will still live together and remain in the marriage. There are marriages where there is little or no sexual intercourse, and the couple may continue to be in a friendly roommate relationship. These marriages are in a minority, but do exist. Some couples even have children after in-vitro pregnancies and may live together in the marriage. There is, of course, shame in such situations, and the secret may never come out. In these cases, the marriage is for the families and the social contract between them, even when it is clear that this contract is not fully honored.

Even in the cases of dating and then love, or a true love marriage, there tends to be more Indian culture involved. This might take the form of the couple's planning the wedding along with their parents, inviting a lot of people their parents are obligated to invite, as well as feeling a lot of pressure for everyone in both families to get along with each other. The couple does count on being fully accepted and welcomed by each other's families, and the shortfall in these relationships can lead to a lot of distress, resulting in depression and conflict. Not being fully accepted by a parental in-law figure tends to have more impact on the couple in the Indian community than in Western culture. There are more expressions of sadness, more efforts made to please, and considerable emotional energy expended on trying to figure out why they are not getting along. The woman is almost always expected to adapt, adjust, and be patient. Elder members of the extended family will often chip in and say things like, "Don't worry, he is like that—a bit difficult to please, but give it time," or "Just try calling her every week and talk about cooking; or ask questions about how your husband was as a child," in an attempt to help everyone get along better, but especially the daughter-in-law get on better with the mother-in-law. This effort reflects the importance of the immediate family, not just the nuclear couple. Although the woman in most cultures is more responsible for the emotional health and social connections of the family, in Indian families the pressure is felt even more intensely, and her ability to manage it has the capacity to strengthen or weaken the family. The mother-in-law holds a lot of power in the relationship, in that she can set the tone for her son and daughter-in-law's happiness by her level of intrusion or support.

I can't emphasize enough that whether the marriage starts as a "love" marriage, a traditional arranged marriage, or something in between, some things don't change. The feelings and pressure of how things should be in the family is unaffected by how the relationship begins. It is as if the families are unconsciously caught up in the system of being matched. Once the parents agree to the match, then the path forward is indistinguishable from that of the traditional arranged marriage. The pull back towards home is like new clothes over old—the foundation garments are still old and have not changed a lot.

CHAPTER SIX

Solpa Adjust Maadee

When on a bus or train in India, a person may request another passenger, "*Solpa adjust Maadee*"—could they please scoot in a little more so four people may sit on the bench seat instead of the three it is meant to hold? Or, could the passenger in a rickshaw make room for another fare who may be going in the same direction? Or, could the tailor modify his schedule and put your clothes ahead in line so you can have them sooner?

"*Solpa adjust Maadee*" is a common phrase in *Kannada* (mixed with a little English) in the language of the South Indian state of Karnataka. *Solpa* means "just a bit," "adjust" is obvious, and *maadee* means "please make or please do." The phrase is often supplemented with an honorific like *swami* [sir], preceded by *deyvittu* [in God's name], or with a physical gesture, like putting all the right-hand fingertips together or the right-hand palm turned up at a 45-degree angle. It is used to make a request of another person when a favor is being asked. The request could also be used to apologize and ask pardon for an inconvenience, by asking for understanding. Clearly, the person to whom the request is made is not under any obligation to grant the favor, although they most often do.

Solpa adjust Maadee is a phrase that asks for wiggle room and incorporates an English word that is itself flexible and widely understood. Wiggle room may not exist in the United States where things are more regulated, and there is less space and time to take from another. In India, space is compressed, and people learn to be genuinely accommodating and share with others. There are four times the number of people in India in one third of the space, compared to the density of the population in the United States. Although there is plenty of physical space in the United States, each person requires more space—each person's personal space is larger and more valued. Most people are also acutely conscious of taking up another person's time, and hesitate before asking for free time.

The concept of sharing more time and space is not something that comes easily to most people in the United States. It does not translate. So most Indians have one standard for their Indian friends and a different one for their non-Indian friends. When invited to a party at an Indian family home, Indians will arrive about half-an-hour to an hour after they have been asked to come and usually stay longer. So, if it is a mixed group, there is some discomfort even before the party has begun—When to arrive? Will the "whites" show up earlier and wait for the Indians to arrive? Should some of the Indians arrive earlier? These are some of the questions the host family has to ponder and manage. It is understood that Middle Easterners, Europeans, and South Americans are different from Americans and more like Indians in the ways that they socialize. Indian people like to sit down for visits, and not stand around and talk. There is an understanding that hospitality includes sitting down to talk—standing around the kitchen only works for very short visits and is seen as very "American" and not genuine or polite enough for true friends. Standing in others' kitchens is viewed as pseudo-intimacy that falsely implies that you are close enough to have cooked together. Sitting together may be more formal but also reflects that you have committed to time together and that you are not about to leave. As one Indian friend put it, "standing, standing, you are thinking of going and speak only little little." This sharing of time and space sometimes divides Indians from Americans.

Given the divide that exists between American culture and other cultures, Indians make an effort to bridge the gap. This effort is reflected in the naming of children. Of the vast set of names available for children in India, there is a smaller subset that is used in the United States. The inability of a large English- (only) speaking population to hear or pronounce the many nuances of sounds in Indian languages is the limiting factor. So, names are tried out to see how mangled they may get when used by Americans. Some very popular names are clever takes on a word that may already be familiar to Americans. For example, the name "Neel" which means blue, is easily pronounceable by the larger population that is used to "Neil." *Saraswati*, the goddess of learning, is shortened to "Sara." Some Indians still hold on to naming their children in the traditional way, using words that cannot be mispronounced—for example, Vaidehi, or Nikhil. A name that is a home-name for a boy—for example, *Vinod*, is usually mispronounced here as "Vi-Nod" while the correct way is "Vee-No-The." The more acculturated the family, the more attention is paid to the careful choice of names. Still other Indians just bite the bullet and find a middle name that is English and use that for all the outside-world interactions. Indian families also creatively use spelling to help names be better pronounced phonetically, not the way the word would be spelled in India. This concept of Americanizing names is sometimes stretched to a breaking point. *Anjali* may be spelled "Unjli" to make it easier to pronounce. This spelling gets laughed at only on visits to India! An acquaintance who introduced himself with "My name is Shivashankar, call me Steve" made both Indians and non-Indians smile in puzzlement because the gap was so huge and dissonant—it just did not work.

Names are not physical spaces, but do convey psychological space. When a person's name is not pronounced right, the psychological space between people gets enlarged. The choice of names for a child who will grow up in this country determines how this space will be bridged. A too short and nondifferentiated name like Suzie makes for a very short gap—it is very homogenized. With too long a name, or one difficult to pronounce, the gap grows uncomfortably large. The adjustments in naming are more than *solpa* [little], and people do mind the gap. A comfortable name, like jeans or comfortable western clothing, makes the issue a non-issue. The space is bridged.

While the naming of pets is not a major event, it is still symbolic and illustrative in a different way. In India, even Hindu people give their dogs Christian names like Tommy, George, Rex, Suzie—or English words like Rocket, Prince, Julie, or Bingo. I have wondered if the practice of using of foreign names for dogs was symbolic of a foreign custom of keeping dogs in the home. Or, was it symbolic of an outsider who did not quite fit into the family? When an Indian family returned to India after living in the United States and named their dog *Krishna*, it certainly raised some eyebrows. Were they making a statement? Were they trying to show that they were different? Were they saying the dog was as Indian as they were, and, by the way, how Indian were they? Were they just being showoffs? Were they saying they were better than the rest of us somehow? No one said anything specific, but this is what I inferred from the half-smiles of discomfort, the half-expressed shakes of the head, and the slow nods. People were certainly puzzled by this reverse cultural expression.

Indians make adjustments to living here in the United States. I also want to acknowledge that, likewise, many, many Americans make adjustments to us. People make efforts to say our foreign names right—names that the brains of people raised with a single Western language have trouble with. Perhaps we Indians are asking the Americans to "please, *solpa adjust maadee*." Most Americans make efforts and express interest in getting to know us, our cultures, and have welcomed us. Even though most of us have encountered some incidents of racism and exclusion, these United States are mostly a welcoming space.

CHAPTER SEVEN

Bracketing the Matrix
—The Caste System

The caste system is an institution that holds a lot of morbid fascination for most Americans, probably because it parallels the segregation of African Americans and the history of slavery in the United States.

The United States is a country that prides itself on equality for all, with an illusion of equal opportunity, and considers its society to have no class boundaries, except for those defined by money. In other words, there is a belief and faith that it is a true meritocracy. Although most people agree that there are "old boys' networks" and some other exclusive networks (through family, social, or religious organizations' connections), it is generally considered possible for people to gain upward mobility within a generation if they can access education and/or make a lot of money. Equal access to a quality education is not so available to a person living in a tenement that is gang-ridden and in a high crime neighborhood as it is to a person in a higher-income neighborhood. Nevertheless, the Indian immigrant community understands that staying in school is the way out and up—from a class/caste system that they would not be able to escape from so easily in India. This mobility within a generation is just beginning to happen within the middle class in certain large cities in India, but even if a person makes a lot of money, caste follows them like a shadow.

The caste system in India has been in existence for thousands of years. It provided social structure and stability but became exploitative and rigid over time and with Colonial influence. The highest caste are the *Brahmins*, or the priests and scholars; the next are the *Kshatriyas*, or the warriors; then the traders or *Vaishyas*; and, the lowest who do menial work are the *Shudras*. Even in the lowest group, the *Dalits* who are outside the caste system, there are subdivisions: those who do specifically assigned menial work (like cleaning and curing animal hides), and those who belong to Scheduled castes or tribes. The Scheduled castes and tribes are the historically disadvantaged groups of people recognized in the Constitution of India and make up almost a quarter of India's population. The Brahmins make up only about five percent of the population, but have held a lot of the power in the past. The caste one is born into determines one's work and station in life, for life's entirety and for the generations to follow. It is rigid, inflexible, and can be discerned by the last name of the family, as well as by some less obvious but perceptible family history and background. Mobility between castes is understood to be something that can only be achieved through death and rebirth—there is a belief is that actions during the current lifetime may dictate the caste one is born into in the next lifetime.

Modern India has tried to address some of the injustices of the rigid caste system by means of a reservation system (similar to affirmative action for education and employment) to help groups of people who have previously faced discrimination. The country has economic, educational, and employment protections in place to help historically disadvantaged peoples get ahead. Although the caste system is still of huge significance in modern India, people of different castes are no longer as rigidly separated in the big cities, where there can be more anonymity and upward mobility for those who get access to education. A person's identity may still be bound by his or her caste while living in India, but less so when living in the United States. In India, there is still much subtle or overt discrimination against the lower castes, even among the urban and educated populations.

Anu and Bala are a young couple with two children. Anu comes from a caste that is not Brahmin. Bala's parents are orthodox Brahmins and religious people who were disappointed when their son chose to marry outside their caste. Bala says that his parents are now at peace with his decision and have accepted his wife and love their precious grandchildren completely. Anu is more sensitive to and conscious of all the undercurrents to which the discriminated-against all over the world are subject. She has never been invited to do the *puja* [prayers and prayer rituals] in the family *puja* room. Her in-laws find creative ways to decline eating at her parents' home, where meat may have been cooked the previous day. There is no way to convince her in-laws that the food would be cooked specially for them in a "pure" way, in separate vessels, and without being polluted by touch. (In most Indian homes and restaurants, non-vegetarian foods are kept in separate dishes and sometimes even on separate tables, so as to not offend the sensibilities of vegetarians.) Bala looks ashamed when Anu talks about it, but he feels helpless because he also understands his parents' reservations and almost physical revulsion against food smells and sights that offend them. Anu and Bala's children may never know these differences if they grow up in the United States. But, in the India of today, these differences are still an unfortunate reality (although less so in the big cities and among more educated "modern" people,) with the problem being worse in rural areas. But how can the reality of the external world not impact Anu's internal world?

It is common for middle and upper class families to have several household helpers who are called servants. In another instance, a family that has treated their servant Kalyani (typically belonging to a lower caste) as a family member accepts the servant completely, allowing and inviting her to take part in puja and in the family's kitchen. They send her to a trade school so that she can better her life and her family's future. They still do have to deal with "knowing" looks and implications made by society that no good can come of this—visitors routinely attempt to put her in her place. Some visitors look askance when she brings food to the table or comes into the living room without the expected obsequious self-effacing gestures. Their attempts to put her in place can range from a sharp look to a gruff "What do you want now?"—even in the presence of the host family.

Caste impacts social interactions differently in the United States.. The families hold onto their customs, beliefs, and values while having to integrate what the children bring into the home in terms of American values: equality and a caste- and class-free society. There are many families who integrate the equality of all beliefs with a sense of freedom and joy, and there are other families who try to convince their children to stay within social circles that the parents define. This might take the form of suggesting that the children look for life partners within the same community of *Patels* or *Iyers* or *Iyengars*. All *Patels* would be expected to have been raised with the same values of that community and at least an exposure to the *Gujarati* language and customs. The values may be of essential higher education, being conscious of frugality and health, and of pride in self-reliance. All Iyers would be expected to have family that would speak a version of Tamil, and Iyengars would be expected to speak either Tamil or Kannada or a mixture of the two. There would also be an expectation of a vegetarian diet in the home and interest in classical South Indian music and dance. So, although the parents have some influence on whom their children marry, especially if they are arranging the marriage, there are circles of preference within the Indian community. An Iyer family may prefer that their child marries into another Iyer family or at lease an Iyengar who would have South Indian values. There are widening circles of what is an acceptable choice within the Indian community. Some of these circles are more permeable than others; and the barriers in society vary according to caste and religion.

Many young people who begin the process of looking for a life partner online look at matrimonial websites like *Telugu Matrimony* or *Tamil Matrimony* that are already narrowed down by language spoken at home. Within that, they narrow their search by their castes and subcastes. This is not an overt discrimination against a person of another caste but a simpler way of finding someone who is culturally similar to them. This funnels down parameters of language, custom, food styles, prayer habits, and value of education and work. Many young folks in college or in the working world will not even consider a person of another religion or caste, because of the implicit idea that the larger family will have to overcome biases to accept the person. Of course there are exceptions—people do marry between religions and castes, but there is a common knowledge that this will make things more difficult. Caste used to define, very rigidly, the conventions in wedding, meals, and religious rites, and is still recognized as a bridge to be crossed with care.

A Brahmin Hindu-Muslim relationship, and a marriage between a Brahmin and a Dalit may be more difficult to navigate. Families will count themselves lucky if their child has a "love marriage" and still marries within the same caste. If their child marries a non-Brahmin, they will console themselves by saying, "At least she is not a Muslim" or "At least he is not a Hindu," finding solace in the contemplation of what could have been worse. Even if the immediate family accepts the outsider, there is an awareness that more orthodox relatives will not accept the outsider and may not invite the person to religious events. The outsiders are always more sensitive to where they are welcome and where they are not. Marriages between people of different castes are still the exception, even when the couple meets by non-traditional means not arranged by the families. However, change does happen over generations and not just years.

People have various beliefs and biases about people of different castes. A gradient of open-mindedness toward equality is influenced by time and living in larger cities. The Brahmins feel superior to people of other castes, and consider their own ways to be best. Some people of non-Brahmin castes think that Brahmins are too restricted in their ways and are cut off from enjoyment of life. A person belonging to the generation who is sixty to eighty at the time of this writing would have been raised with more inflexible beliefs. A person who is in his or her forties to sixties at the time of this writing would have been raised with their parents' beliefs about differences and separation, but with more exposure to, and association with, people of various castes, and so they are more likely to be open-minded.

Prasad is a marketing manager at a large corporation and his children are studying at universities. His daughter is dating a Jewish young man in New York, and Prasad is happy she has found a stable and family-oriented person. His wife is sad about what she perceives will be lost—traditions and religious practices that will doubtless be abandoned. Prasad and his wife are related—their parents were cousins.

Prasad's father lived in big cities, worked in the United Nations, and, as a child, Prasad traveled and saw many different countries and cultures. Prasad's wife's father was raised in a small village in Kerala where the caste lines were clearly defined. Prasad's wife recalls that when she was a child, the workers who came to labor in their fields would stand a respectful 10-15 feet away from her father as they talked with him so that the possibility of even their shadows touching her father was minimized. Never had a person of a different caste come into her house (except to clean) until she left India. She was raised to believe that non-Brahmins were "dirty" and polluted by eating meat, drinking alcohol, and not being raised with "clean" habits. Her cousins, if and when faced with meeting Prasad's potential Jewish son-in-law, would have varying degrees of comfort in their encounters with him. Some would only know he was "a white man," some would understand him to be "a Jew" and make associations with the Jewish populations in Kerala—a microscopically small community that is still evident by the presence of a few synagogues and regarded by the majority population as a curiosity. The daughter's cousins who live in the United States would only know that "he is sort of Jewish, right? And his parents might want them to get married in their temple?" The daughter's generation is less judging, more accepting, and generally more ignorant of all the differences between people.

I view the caste system as an environment in which life in India develops, and, it is a matrix or structure that stratifies the experience of one's life. It was easier for me to live my life in India being bracketed as part of the upper castes that (along with family fortunes) had access to more resources. I was not discriminated against on the basis of my caste in any obvious way, but was probably not able to get some of the "reserved for Scheduled Castes and Tribes" spots in some institutions or colleges. If one sets aside the question of the real existence of the caste system—it really cannot exist outside of India or out of its context, as it has no objective nature apart from a probable lineage of a few hundreds of years—it is a subjectively experienced phenomenon and can only be put into perspective as such. Asking persons how they experience their caste and sect as it impacts their relationships would be a good place to begin to understand how they are affected by their inherited position in society.

The above examples are not to say that there aren't many families that have shed all the baggage that comes with caste and religion. There are. And equality for all is the hope outwardly expressed by leaders of the country and inwardly believed in and held by those who are idealistic. I would like to believe that progress is rapid but must consider that people's experiences often belie that.

CHAPTER EIGHT

Christmas in June
—The Summer Visits

For many immigrant Indians, April showers bring more than May flowers. Around this time each year, physicians I know routinely hand out more than the usual number of prescriptions (anti-depressants and anti-anxiety medication) to their Indian patients. There are more cases of headaches, stomach issues, sleeplessness, strain, anxiety, fear, and other symptoms of stress. Along with the increase in doctor's office visits, there is also a higher incidence of difficulties among couples.

The annual summer visit home to India is emotionally tumultuous. There are tickets to buy, homes to be locked up, presents to be bought, and, most important, decisions and emotional discussions about where to stay and when. The in-law issues in many families set the mood for the whole trip. Who will be upset, who needs to be placated, and who needs to be dealt with firmly are decisions easier to make when the couple acts as a unit. When there are divisions between husband and wife, the trip home becomes a minefield to be navigated with extreme caution.

Going home to a welcoming mother is obviously very different from going home to a stern, demanding, or unfriendly mother-in-law. The relationship between the mother-in-law and the daughter-in-law then becomes the gateway to war or peace between the couple and both families. When family is everything, fostering a good relationship between both families is even more than everything. The politics of negotiating the intricacies of who-owes-whom-what makes international diplomacy between world powers seem like child's play. The following questions show the thoughtfulness with which such matters are handled: Have all the people who matter been invited? Will there be hurt feelings for anyone? Have gifts been reciprocated as expected? Will there be enough extra gifts in case we have forgotten someone?

If a whole extended family is invited to an event at a home or hotel, seating and food are worried over, but scant attention is paid to the décor of the venue. The quality of the food is very important, and the honoring of the guests is of utmost importance. The hosts make sure the guests are seated and that the food served is enough, ask everyone several times if they would like more, and pay a lot of attention to the comfort of the guests. The daughter-in-law is expected to be a hostess even if she is visiting. The whole extended family is assumed to be watching and judging the relationship to assess the balance of power and harmony. The daughter-in-law is told, subtly and directly, that she is in charge of good feelings for the whole family. While this may be an easy task in a family where there is already harmony and positive feeling, it is an almost impossible task where there are difficulties.

The husband feels honor-bound to support his parents, especially his mother, and cannot afford to appear to agree with his wife's version of events, even if he does. Too often, he is caught in the web of expectations and gets flak from both sides—his wife and his mother. In most families, there is the expectation of equal time being spent at both sets of parents' homes. In very traditional families, the wife is expected to spend more time at her in-laws' home (married home) and very little time at her parents' home (birth home). It may be accepted in these more traditional families that the husband visits his in-laws for a very brief period and that there is more formality in the relationship between the husband and his in-laws. The formality follows the expectation that the son-in-law is an honored guest and must be pleased at all costs. If he is kept happy, the likelihood that he will treat his wife with kindness increases. He is higher up in the social hierarchy than his wife.

As a couple negotiates an understanding of how they will manage visits, the first few visits home may define the relationship for the couple. There are many families who take months and sometimes years to recover from the stress of a trip back home or from the parents' visit to them. Small events get blown up and out of proportion when respect or disrespect for in-laws is involved—whether it is implied or real.

Meena and her husband Nikhil went to visit family during the summer. The agreement was that they would stay at Nikhil's home for the first half of the visit. Their baby was a year old and Nikhil's parents had not spent much time with the baby. When they stayed at Nikhil's home, Meena tried her best to please her in-laws. She cooked, helped with the housework, and took care of the baby. Although Nikhil's parents were willing to help, they did not appreciate Meena's helpful hints about what the baby liked and didn't like. Misunderstandings compounded rapidly. The baby was going through a phase of stranger anxiety, so he cried every time his grandparents tried to pick him up. The apartment was noisy and baby and mother struggled with jet lag. Nikhil was not around a whole lot. He went out with friends he had not seen in many years, leaving Meena and the baby in what he assumed were good hands. Meena was caught between wanting to please Nikhil's family and anger at Nikhil for leaving her at home without his help. She did not want to complain to Nikhil about his parents. Nikhil was puzzled—there were two more people to help with the baby—why did Meena need him? He failed to grasp the complexity of the expectations society and his parents had of Meena. He could not identify with Meena's anger. He could not put himself in her place.

When the family went to stay at Meena's parents' home, he saw a different Meena. She was relaxed, happy, went out with friends, and the baby seemed happier too. More important, Meena's parents waited on Nikhil, and tried hard to make him comfortable and happy. Meena is unwilling to visit India again with Nikhil and refuses to renew her passport and visa. She wants several things made clear to Nikhil—she needs him to be with her throughout the visit to his parents' home, and also to help out when they visit her home. She is looking for a more equitable relationship, but one that the parent generation does not yet accept or understand. When the dynamics were explained to Nikhil as a sociological construct, he was more willing to accept what Meena wanted. When

Meena naively talked about his parents and Meena's dislike of how much was expected of her, Nikhil became defensive and felt compelled to take his parents' side.

Many Indian men assume, mistakenly, that their wives will speak up when upset by in-law interactions. Many Indian women assume that their husbands can see and hear what they view as unequal treatment by the in-laws. Sometimes couples need an explicit review of social constructs in Indian families, especially those that were set in their parents' times and that their parents still adhere to. It would be hugely beneficial to both parties if there were clear expectations discussed before the wedding. Premarital counseling is not something that is part of Hindu lifestyle and religion. When there is trouble, the couple approaches an aunt or uncle, who is often able to talk to the couple about how to please both sets of parents. In the last ten to fifteen years, the number of women who are educated, and hold on to jobs and careers in the outside world, has increased hugely. These women are unwilling to bow to unfair demands on them and more willing to face a breakup leading to divorce.

There are many, many families where the old ways still hold. The wife is expected to be a good daughter-in-law, pleasing everyone. The husband is an honored guest at his in-laws' home. The difference is that even when the women agree to live with the old rules, or have no choice but to agree, they hold a simmering anger against the system that boils over onto their husbands. Indians have changed many ideas, ways, and beliefs, but this special treatment for the son-in-law is a stronghold. Indian men have often been raised to revere their mothers—his mother is sacred and he is supposed to defend her at all costs. When the built-in inequality of the system is pointed out to the men as a sociological construct, these men are less defensive and better able to hear the women's side of things. In these situations, men have often taken their privileges for granted and, being embedded in tradition, cannot see outside their immediate family of origin.

In families where the mother and father do not get along, it may have become the son's role to keep the mother happy. In many such families, the mother is less willing to share her son with the new daughter-in-law, and there are greater difficulties between the mother-in-law and daughter-in-law. The son feels caught in the middle and does not take sides, angering both women, or takes his mother's side and abandons his wife. This is the stuff of many unhappy families and addressed in numerous *saas-bahu* (mother-in-law daughter-in-law) television serials in India.

Meanwhile, back in the U.S.A., the parents are coming! Every year, just before summer begins, most parents in the United States start thinking about summer camps, holidays, longer days, and plans to manage their children's time when they may be at work. A parallel process goes on in many South Asian homes—are the parents coming for the summer? This is of huge significance in the lives of the families in this community.

In some families there is secret groaning, in others great anticipation and joy, and in still others relief that there will be family help to manage children who may not need to be sent to camps after all. For all in this equation, the quality of life changes considerably. There is a rich mixture of emotions, work, play, relaxation, and relief that goes into this amalgam that it is worthy of comment and study.

Geeta and Harish are a couple from North India with two children who are thirteen and eight. Geeta works part-time as an occupational therapist with seniors and Harish is a hardware engineer whose company is threatening layoffs, although Harish does not seem too worried about it. Harish's parents are expected for the summer to help out with the children and enjoy a break from the monotony of their lives in India. Geeta and Harish come in to see me because their normally good relationship is very strained and they are afraid their children are affected badly by their quarrels.

Harish's parents are in their seventies and retired. Harish and their other son are well settled in life but live outside India. Harish's parents have not found a second purpose in life and they feel unmoored, unwanted, and possibly used by their children. When they come to visit Harish, they face their own waning importance in their children's and grandchildren's worlds.

Geeta's parents died fifteen years ago in a tragic accident, and Harish's parents are her closest parental figures. Even so, she feels a tremendous strain every summer when Harish's parents come to visit for three to five months, which is the average length of stay for most parents in the community. The duration of the visit has evolved to this figure based on U.S. visa regulations, airline ticket validity, length of summer vacation for children, weather in the United States, the distance and time for travel, and on the intangible meaning and value of paying so very much for the tickets.

"The whole house turns upside down and I can barely function," says Geeta with a nervous glance at her husband. "I love them, but it is a strain," she adds guiltily. "I feel terrible saying this because they help with the children, they are such nice people, and I do love them." She looks at Harish to see how he reacts. Harish leans back and surprises her by agreeing that it is difficult for him, too, even though they are his parents. He finds reasons to come home later or to leave earlier for work, and the coming layoff worries him in a different way than it does Geeta. Geeta adds that she wishes she could work longer hours if Harish could pick up the slack at home for a few months. She is resentful of the weeklong hiking trip that he has planned with a group of male friends, and also ashamed of her feelings of wanting to escape.

The children's reactions are mixed. The eight-year-old is thrilled to have grandparents read with him and play with him everyday, but the thirteen-year-old is angry at having to share space with the grandparents. "I miss being just the four of us and they don't understand me," he admitted to his father in a surprising and rare expression of actual feelings.

Counterintuitively, in families where there is outright hostility between the parent generation and the in-laws coming to visit, things may actually go more smoothly. Everyone knows how everyone else feels and the writing is on the wall, clear for all to see. In such families, there is an expectation that the visit be managed and carefully negotiated with compromises all around, so that there are no explosive incidents. This was not the situation with Harish and Geeta.

Worry is the next chapter in Geeta and Harish's lives—for how will they deal with aging parents far away, whom will they be indebted to, whose scorn and anger will they face, and how much complication will come from migrating to this faraway golden world? Harish sometimes wakes up with nightmares—a late-night call from India, a hurried trip home, having to deal with his extended family in India, and grief even in the thick of the dream. Harish is more aware of the fragility of his parents' brave faces and knows what it means to owe a debt to his extended family in India. The cousins and uncles are the ones whom his parents have to call to alert them of ill health or when they have to be admitted to a hospital. The cousins and aunts and uncles keep a close eye on his parents. Harish and Geeta are grateful for their care and acknowledge it each time they visit. They feel bad that Harish's parents compromise on some of their values or beliefs in the larger interest of keeping peace and relationships smooth. For example, when an aunt is snippy and rude, they ordinarily may turn down the next couple of invitations to events at the aunt's home, feigning an illness or some other commitment. After a couple of refusals, the aunt then will come over with an excuse of dropping something off and will make sure she is extra friendly and polite. After hints have been dropped and taken, relationships will resume normally. But, because both their children are far away, his parents do not use the tools they would have and, instead, swallow their pride and put up with the aunt's rudeness. Harish and Geeta see this, know it, put up with it, and extend their parents' indebtedness by being sure to thank family members for taking extra care in their absence.

Harish and Geeta are both usually glad to leave India after a visit with all the emotional heavy lifting involved. They wish his parents would come and settle down near them and be supported by their two grown children, but their parents are loath to make long-term plans that involve a change of countries at their (according to them, advanced) age. Harish and Geeta are unable to communicate their worry in a way that would make sense to their parents. Harish tries to tell them it is easier to move now than when there is only one of them left, but it upsets them, and he has given up trying. Being judged by relatives in India who assume Harish and Geeta live in the United States "just for money only"—relatives, moreover, who do not know the stresses and ease of life in this country—is exhausting for the couple. So, with all these emotions floating around and brought home more sharply on each parental visit, it is no wonder that Harish and Geeta feel the strain of the coming summer visit.

When parents come to visit for the summer, Geeta feels the strain more than Harish, even though she has a great relationship with her in-laws. She maintains the social calendar, plans sightseeing trips and weekend parties, keeps the pantry stocked, keeps the children busy and active, and stays in touch with her friends. In discussing her stress with Harish, she realizes that, although they all have good relationships with Harish's parents, she also works very hard to keep it that way. Geeta has the other set of parents that most Indian women are raised to expect in their lives, but she admits that they are not her parents in a way that she could have kicked back and relaxed with. Geeta misses her parents.

Even if Harish and Geeta live in a nuclear family, the family life in India that Harish's parents have must be taken into account. The emotional reach of the extended family is always present as a penumbra, casting a steadying and intertwining influence on the nuclear family. The nuclear family is still indebted to the extended family, and this is part of the structure of taking favors from relatives that costs a couple some freedoms. This "lena-dena" [give-and-take] reaches out over the miles and is part of the price paid when there is no sibling living in India to take care of the parents. If there were a sibling living in India close to or with the parents, life would be easier for this couple in America. Everyone would sleep better at night. Of course one is indebted to the sibling in India, but that is easier than not having a sibling there at all to help care for aging parents.

Harish's situation is complicated by the fact that his brother has married a European woman. She is a charming, outspoken, and strong German woman. Everyone agrees that she is easy to get along with and has a loving heart. But, according to Harish, "It is just not the same as having an Indian sister-in-law. I feel my parents will never say it, but I don't think they are okay staying with my brother and sister-in-law for a long time." It is an undercurrent, seldom openly expressed, that a son or daughter-in-law who comes from another culture will not be as willing to sacrifice and take care of aging older relatives. It may be an unfair assumption about Indian vs. non-Indian, but it does exist. So Harish believes his parents will ultimately settle down with him—that this is his duty to them and what he believes to be the correct thing to do—his

Dharma. "It will be an adjustment when they finally move in with us, but we will have their grace and blessing" is Harish and Geeta's acceptance of the situation. "The children are not used to having them here all the time, and we don't expect our children to care for us like we care for our parents. What to do—the children are American." Geeta and Harish are the sandwich generation, caught between two age groups, two cultures, and two worlds.

Summers for the Indian immigrant community can be as nuanced and complex as Christmas and Thanksgiving for the rest of the country.

CHAPTER NINE

Crossed Wires—ABCD and FOB

A n eager atmosphere envelops the high school gym as volunteer parents of the new freshman class gather to plan one of the first social events of the year. While it is clear there are small knots of parents who know each other, there are several who hang about trying to break the ice and introducing themselves to others in the smaller groups to which they are assigned.

Maya, young-looking, fit, with sleekly groomed hair, is a trendily dressed woman who is quite at ease with herself. She carries a fashionable bag and sunglasses. Easily mistaken for a college student, she is a pharmaceutical representative for a company that is known for making anti-depressants. Meena is another mother in the group, looking around somewhat anxiously for a friendly face. She is new to the area and eager to make a few friends. Meena wears the tiniest possible black speck in the middle of her forehead—a nod to the traditional larger red kumkum or bindi. Her hair is awkwardly styled, neither a short flattering style nor the longer style that can be braided out of the way in the fashion conventional to Indian beauty. Her jeans look a few sizes too large, her running shoes seem styled for men, and her sweatshirt is possibly her son's. Meena can be seen as a person who might be more comfortable in Indian clothes. (Some recent immigrants take several years to understand fashion in the United States. They may look really elegant in their Indian clothes, but look very awkward in western wear, choosing younger fashion that is too youthful and casual for social or work situations. It is more noticeable in women, as the men quickly adopt the long trousers and full sleeved shirts they may wear in India too.) In short, Meena looks the polar opposite of Maya.

Yet, Meena approaches Maya with friendly hope just because she recognizes Maya's Indian features and skin color. "You must be new also," she says by way of introducing herself. Maya's response is a neutral "Aren't we all?" And thus begin the crossed wires. In truth, these women have a lot in common but also a lot that divides them. Meena continues with, "What is your child's last name?" and looks a little taken aback when Maya responds with "Smith." Meena nevertheless persists, "Your child must be doing speech and debate? Or at least Robotics?" She makes a last attempt to connect politely with Maya. These two school activities are understood by most South Asian immigrants to be solid academic choices for their children to add to their portfolios, increasing their advancement towards a good college education. To this, all Maya can say is that her child's activities are yearbook and cheerleading.

If asked, Maya might have said that she is a polite person and did not want to be rude to Meena, but that Meena might as well be from another planet—they have nothing in common. Meena's expectations of another Indian woman were different —Maya should have agreed that she was new there, too, and then explained that she was married to a Caucasian, and, yes, what to do, her child should have been in Robotics or speech and debate, but that she can't help it that her child is willful and not very mature. This would be a culturally appropriate way of relating. Maya might have related better if Meena had said something about how difficult it is to keep their teens from constantly texting while doing homework or something more neutral about the high school experience. Meena got immediately personal in the way that many people in India would—by establishing a knowledge of each other, understanding what language, which city, how many children, where parents are, etc.

Maya has a Western cultural aspect to her manner of speaking, while Meena's manner of speaking is very Indian. In fact, Meena is well-educated, and very confident in her work, education, and family life. She has a Ph.D. in organic chemistry and works as a senior research chemist in the same company that Maya represents. She tells me that she is very drawn to people like Maya—people who seem polished and sophisticated on the surface—but is often rebuffed by them when she makes friendly overtures. She attributes this treatment to the gap between ABCDs and FOBs. ABCDs—American-Born Confused Desis—are the generation that was born and raised in the United States. The immigrant generation considers them—including their own children—to be slightly confused about their identities as Desi [from the home country]. In turn, ABCDs and others consider the immigrant generation—including their own parents—to be Fresh Off the Boat—FOBs. As caricatures usually do, both pejorative identifiers have a large element of truth.

In terms of acculturation, a divide occurs that some more than others are interested in crossing. The people in these separate camps do have different experiences. The ABCDs have had the differentiating and formative experience of going through adolescence in this country—a time where identity as a minority and peer pressure shape many of their experiences. The term *Desi* is inclusive in that it includes people whose origins are from India, Pakistan, Bangladesh and Sri Lanka. The FOBs have a different cultural process—immigration, and then the struggle or excitement of acclimating to the different people and processes of this country. The FOBs view the ABCDs as unable and unwilling to take the risks and make the kinds of sacrifices that the FOBs had to make. The FOBs think the ABCDs have it easy and don't fully appreciate the difficulties of coming of age as easily recognizable immigrants. Stories abound of comical and difficult times and incidents—stories that have at their core the conflict, struggle, pride, and camaraderie that binds this group.

Meena's push-and-pull relationship with people like Maya is a gap she hopes to bridge through persistence and open questioning. She understands that this is the same gap that will occur between her and her teenage daughter, who is, after all, another ABCD. She says that many of her Indian immigrant friends, who are now scattered all over the country, say that ABCDs are rude, that they assume that the FOBs know nothing that is not in the textbooks and are plainly confused. FOBs see their ABCD counterparts as arrogant and scornful, but sometimes to be pitied "because, poor things, they have not grown up in India after all." Meena says it is a stereotype and "people must be assessed on a case by case basis," but is obviously frustrated by encounters such as the one with Maya. "We are from the same place, and maybe I have more in common with her mother, but why can't we get along and help each other?" is what Meena seems to say.

I understand these terms "ABCD" and "FOB" as umbrella terms that encompass a whole world of different experiences. They could just as easily stand for "American-Born Confident Desis" and their "Fearless Obviously Brethren." It takes great courage and drive to leave your country to find a new life in a foreign place.

The divide between ABCD and FOB is clear, but there are other more ambiguous differences *within* the FOB generation. FOBs have an inherent need for stratifying and slotting people into different categories that, as Indian immigrants, they have packed into their baggage and brought with them into this new world. In my parents' younger days, people were expected to mingle within their larger extended family, and therefore caste and culture were uniform within the social group. This was the norm in India although there were families who went outside the norm and invited people of different castes into their homes. These friendships, often based on a common interest like cricket or cards, usually lasted a long, long time and soon the entire families became friends, too. The unspoken bond within these family friends is based on the assumption that if one broke the norms for social mingling, and went out of the family's comfort zone, the friendship must be true. There might even have be gratitude from the family lower down on the social scale that the higher caste family broke with convention to keep the friendship.

After moving to the United States, many Indian people still feel a great need to put people into a class or slot. In my opinion, this need is rigid, but the parameters fluctuate. There's an almost constant assessing and reassessing, sorting and resorting, that goes on in the minds of the people who have this urge to stratify. The parameters are no longer just caste. The sorting goes on with the new markers of wealth—city of residence, private school vs. public school, universities attended, job title and function, and type of cars owned.

Vijaya was hurt and angry after the last mothers' group meeting. At the time, however, she had only been mildly embarrassed. As a young stay-at-home mother, she had been looking forward to making friends with other young Indian mothers. She could pinpoint the exact moment Jaya, the potential friend, had lost interest in her. It was when she revealed the name of the city she lived in. At the first few mothers' group meetings at the hospital, she and Jaya had laughed and chatted with each other, exchanged phone numbers, and Vijaya had looked forward to the next group meeting. Vijaya cycled through feelings of puzzlement, disbelief, anger, hurt, and then disgust. At the end of the final meeting, Vijaya turned away towards a neutral "white" person when Jaya stopped to say goodbye. Vijaya now wonders if she is guilty of the same dismissive behavior, and resolves to make sure that does not happen.

This encounter is an often heard and felt story among those more finely tuned to the nuances of social interaction in the Indian community. Even when people are considered to have "made it," and families are living within the same upscale city, there are fine differences based on whose property is in a more expensive neighborhood. Indian immigrants tend to be acutely aware of their place in the pecking order and socialize more comfortably with their social equals. This hyperawareness of place in an imagined and real hierarchy has an impact on social relationships, both within and between families. Teenagers who are already aware of "coolness" factors are often caught in their parents' social circles and challenge their parents' assumptions, pointing out the inherent snobbery in their relationships. Adult families think and rethink invitations from other Indian families— can they reciprocate in an equal manner? Can they be comfortable with each other? Or will there have to be a small joking reference to their own humble dwellings to let everyone know that the differences are acknowledged and that the social order is still adhered to? These thoughts are, of course, not always consciously considered, just as every invitation to social events is not clearly thought out. Rather, it is an undercurrent that plays a part in social situations.

When American-born-and-raised Uma married Tilak, a man who was raised in India and moved to the United States as a teen, some of these issues created tension between the couple as they tried to find friends they could agree upon. Uma liked several people who had a wide variation in income levels. She seemed equally comfortable with all of them. Tilak felt differently and was reluctant to invite or accept invitations from those who were too many levels above or below their own perceived level. As this was discussed, Uma accused her husband of snobbery and classism. Tilak felt unable to defend his thoughts until a discussion on social structure and niceties of interactions freed him up to think about what choices he was making by narrowing their circle of friends.

Within a group of Indians, there is often an assumption that it is all right to make racist comments. The idea of offending another Indian person does not seem to be considered with any seriousness. When homophobic or racial slurs (mostly about African Americans, whole ethnic groups such as the Chinese, or people of a certain skin color) are made at a party, most people do not speak up and say, "Hey, we are brown, and it hurts to be discriminated against." A lone brave voice may pipe up, but is often discounted, ridiculed, or avoided. This rarely breaks up the party. And it does not follow that the person who was upset and offended stops socializing with the group. The family is too important to discount. If you don't go to the parties and reciprocate, the invitations will stop too and then where *does* one belong? This is peer pressure *desi*-style. The generation that has grown up here does not share these biases, but feels helpless to contradict or call these views out for what they are.

The larger family group takes care of its own. A friend told me of the way he traveled across the United States, driving from one college town to another. As a young student trying to see the country, he rarely checked into a hotel. All he did was drive into University towns at a reasonable time, look in the phone book (those were days when there were phone books) and call a couple of Indian sounding names. He would ask politely if he could crash on their couch and the answer, according to him, was always yes. Invariably, he was also offered dinner and breakfast. Another example of group cooperation is when a few Indian students graduating the same year got together and decided on the most practical car they could buy. They picked a make and model, and when they all got jobs, bought five cars of the same make and model at a discounted price from the dealer. Practicality won over individual likes and preferences when careers and lives were just starting. In India, when most Indians make big purchases, or even small ones, it is common to consult with family and friends and take their opinion into valued consideration before making decisions. It is more common to use social networks than search engines.

The status consciousness reflects an intense competition between and among families of Indian immigrants. It is almost as if most of us are not interested in competing with other racial groups, but really only looking over our shoulders at our Indian peers. But some things supersede competition—especially the care of children. Neighbors take extra care of their Indian neighbors' kids. As an unspoken and unbroken rule, the parents know that they can depend on each other to feed the children and care for them if one of them is late. Indians depend on Indian neighbors in a way that they rarely depend on any other neighbor—another mutually supportive network.

The Indian network in the United States is now more powerful than it was twenty years ago. The complex set of connections has morphed into an effective functional association that can help one get jobs, get support within a company, share lunch, indulge in insider trading, and serve the purpose of a "mafia" or a mutually supportive clique. As with any other clique, its powers can be used for both good and bad. A social group of Indians is essential to the mental health and wellbeing of most Indians, as it is a reflecting pool, a source of emotional warmth and sustenance, a resource for financial information and essential knowledge, as well as a wellspring to sustain and increase Indian culture and values.

As the diaspora has grown, it is no longer a single unit—its identity has begun to fragment. There are gradations within the group depending on when the person arrived, where s/he was born, and whether s/he came to study or work. The crossed wires are between these subgroups. As the Indian community continues to invest their lives and put down roots in the United States, I expect the crossed wires will continue to intermingle, but also form an active network of support.

CHAPTER TEN

Vitamins for Better Health

M ohan and Gayu (short for Gayathri) are a quirky-looking couple in their forties. Gayu is dressed in a very '60's style with Birkenstocks, socks, clothes for an active life style that include zip-off at the knees trousers and fleece jackets. She says it is a matter of pride to her that all her clothes will fit in a suitcase. She has cultivated such a minimalist lifestyle by thinking carefully about things they need, and only buying those things, not the things they want and could have. The exceptions, she says, are "fresh flowers and children." She almost bounces on her toes as she walks, and this says a lot about her—she is full of energy, love of life, and curiosity.

Mohan is a huge man—six feet or taller, laid back, peaceful, even-tempered, with a ready grin. He wears neatly pressed cotton slacks and a formal shirt with sleeves rolled up. When Gayu talks about her clothes, he gestures to his own and admits he is a little more vain, but wears his "work uniform" with modish style. He confesses that he is a "management type" and has been very successful, rising up fairly rapidly in a large multinational consulting company. His more than adequate income makes it easy for them to provide their children with the best private school education, while Gayu works from home designing and maintaining websites for architects.

Mohan and Gayu consulted me to talk about their son who is eleven years old. They describe him as active, bright-eyed, curious, and highly sensitive. Gayu describes the relationship between Mohan and their child as becoming tense. It used to be "fantastic and fun all the time" but has now become something that keeps her on edge. Mohan says that is Gayu's problem and that he sees no problem at all. He says she interferes too much in the relationship between father and son.

The very fact that they came to consult me at this stage is completely atypical of South Asian culture. There has been no doctor recommendation, no illness, no big fights, no one, quite literally, falling over, no counseling suggested by the school, and no talk of divorce. Ordinarily, going to a therapist is highly stigmatized and speaks of failure, secrets, and shame. Mohan and Gayu's little family is fairly happy and well-adjusted. What they want is more, better, and far-sighted prevention of a potentially difficult time. Gayu says she has heard from friends in the Indian community that many of the women dread the "'tween" and teenage years as a time of intense conflict between fathers and sons.

When I ask Gayu and Mohan how and why they thought of therapy, they exchange a look and say that Mohan's cousin is a psychoanalyst and suggested some family therapy to prevent a problem. They have insider information! For a clear-thinking and organized couple such as Mohan and Gayu, prevention of a problem in their most vital and key relationships is a high priority.

It is comparatively easy to love and manage a young child, but as that child gets to the teenage years, the relationship can get more complex and difficult. This situation is also impacted by the kind of relationship the father had with his own father. In many Indian families, women dread the almost inevitable conflict between father and son during the son's teenage years. It may be hearsay, but, according to many of these families, Western families are different in that the mother-daughter relationship is the one that is feared and seen as the more difficult one during teenage years or even after. According to one Indian woman I interviewed, "Those people don't worship their mothers like we do." She was puzzled by the casual way her American neighbor said, "My mom's a nasty piece of work." The woman I interviewed was emphatic when she said, "*We* never talk like that." When Western women talk about their mothers, there's an almost "shared smile and raised eyebrow" quality to their exchange, as if to say "You know how it is, don't you?" This is more like the exchange between Indian women when they talk about their mothers-in-law. When Indian men talk about their fathers, which is a rare occurrence, there is more likely to be silence or minimal exchange about work he did or his physical health. Among the generation now in their thirties to fifties, fathers are remote presences in their sons' lives, physically present, but in a reserved, formal, and removed way. The father is still the head of the home and, whether nominal or not, he is treated that way.

The "indirect way" is prized and culturally appropriate in many situations. When one is upset with another, the traditional Indian way is to have a third party tell the first one. Direct conflict or communication can be a loss of face and seen as too confrontational. Within the family, this form of communication seems to be typical between father and son. The mother is often the go-between, imparting important information to each. In my opinion, the teenage years are sometimes a transition from one form of communication to the other—from direct contact between father and son, into difficult communication, and then into indirect communication through the mother. The women have a more difficult time during this period and value peace and even preferably lack of communication between father and son. The indirect way may be interpreted as divisive and controlling according to Western culture and graceful according to the Indian way. In families that live according to very traditional Indian values, the teenage years of a son's life are viewed as "boys are like that, what to do?" while the father steps back and away. In the families that are more mixed culturally, there seem to be more tensions during the teenage years, because the families are struggling not only with the teenage period but also with trying to manage the relationship in a culturally different way to make for more closeness.

In Mohan and Gayu's family, the couple have worked on understanding their separate and different heritages of fatherhood and have bridged the gap, bringing that understanding into a new and stronger relationship between father and son, and between husband and wife. They are opting for the best of both families—more direct, affectionate, coach-

and mentor-like and less distant, reserved, and traditional. They have used therapy like vitamins—essential in small quantities, especially when there is a deficiency, for their improved and combined health.

CHAPTER ELEVEN

The Recent Immigrant and Friendships —To Be Understood as To Understand

When I first arrived in this country to go to graduate school, I fell into an instant community. The apartment building I moved into had eight one-bedroom units. Of these, five were occupied by Indian graduate students studying in various departments of the university—mostly engineering and computer science, but also a small number in biology, chemistry, and education. I soon got into the rhythm of studying, cooking, shopping, and leisure—almost always as part of the group. Often, food was cooked in one apartment and everyone (the Indians in the building) ate there. We all ate at each other's homes and treated our new friends like extended family. There was one vacuum cleaner (bought at a yard sale for $1, I was told) that was shared, and very often we all watched TV shows on the small black and white unit together. Only two of the students had cars, and when they went shopping or did laundry, so did everyone else who needed a ride. Rides to the airport and back were of course the smallest part of the sharing. The occupants of the other two non-Indian apartments were invited now and then, but I don't remember them inviting us back except for occasional drinks.

One evening an unfamiliar car pulled up, and a young Indian stranger asked if he could sleep on our couch. He had taken a few months off to travel all over the country. He would stop at university towns and drive around until he found some fellow Indians. He said he would ask to sleep in one of the people's homes, had not been denied a night's sleep ever, but always made friends whom he invited to come visit him. Invariably, he was also offered dinner, and he then took everyone out for ice cream. This is an example of the strength and resilience of the Indian identity and social network system and how quickly and easily it gets created. There were situations where this system was abused, but these were far and few in between.

My experience of graduate school in America says much about the shared values of Indian people, although we students were all from various castes, communities, languages, and parts of India. There was a shared sense of adventure, happiness, camaraderie, and us-versus-U.S. Many of this group had a few friends from other cultures, some dated non-Indians, and some married non-Indians, but, to all of us Indians in that building, home was less far away because of this sense of home that came with living close to other Indians. There was a feeling of generosity, acceptance, and belonging with a group in a strange place where most of us had no roots. This was the good news. The other more private side of recent immigration was the utter sadness of missing close family and being so far away from them. International phone calls 25 years ago were prohibitively expensive, yet it was not unheard of to spend a third or fourth of a bare-bones student income on them. Students sometimes did without medical insurance so they would have money for phone calls home. Many of the young people cried every weekend after too-brief phone calls home; some could not bear the separation and returned to India; some became very depressed and studied minimally; and others got physically ill. The ones that became clinically depressed rarely got appropriate help—there was not a general awareness of the difficulty of leaving home among the American doctors, who assumed that going to college was the same for this group as it was for other students at a college. There was not a sense of being able to go back and see family at the end of the term. Most of us knew we could not afford to go back for at least two full and very long years. There was an understanding among many that the first six months were going to be the most difficult. For Indians who are used to sunny weather and close family interactions, this sometimes became a bleak time that could not be navigated. There was a family and social expectation of financial success, so there was pressure not to return until that could be accomplished. Friendships were and continue to be a substitute for family.

I did make non-Indian friends at the University. Of these, one particular couple built a great friendship with my husband and me. We were well-suited to each other, had similar likes and interests, were well-read in the same areas, and, most importantly, had a shared sense of hospitality. They cooked for us and we for them. I loved them.

When they traveled to visit family in another part of the country, they asked if I would housesit and care for their dog. I was happy to do so because I loved dogs, missed my own, and, besides, they were generous hosts, leaving me treats and goodies that they had baked for me. Mostly, I did it because they were my friends, and it was easy for me. But when they returned, we got into a friendship-breaking situation. The husband of the couple insisted on paying me with painstakingly baked bread that he knew I loved. Most importantly, he used the word "payment" and I, very naturally, refused. I said I needed no payment, I had not helped for pay, and I did not need to be paid because we were friends. Moreover, I would expect them to help me out in the future if they could, not because I took care of their dog but because friends help one another. He was hurt because I refused his food, and I was upset that he would not see my point. I said I ate at their home "all the time" and did not need to be paid and, if he would give me the bread "just because," I would take it. He was too angry and hurt to talk to me for a few days and I remember crying over it. We eventually talked it over, and he and his wife and I tried to repair our friendship. But I was leaving in a few months, as they were, and it was never the same again. I write this with lingering sadness as I fully expected us to be friends for life in the way it would have been with an Indian family friendship.

This incident was the first one that showed me the difference between Indian and American friendships. I was too proud of my values, young, more hotheaded than I am now, and ignorant of American values to be able to put the differences aside for the moment. My friend did not want to "owe" me and I wanted him to acknowledge that he could not pay for my friendship. I was naïve and immature, and not gracious enough to take the bread and let things be to talk over at a later time. I also realize I was interacting with them in the way I would have with Indian friends, where there is less emphasis on formal thanking and saying sorry. Indian friendships tend to be more intense, verging on the rude (as interpreted in American culture) and expressions of "Don't be stupid *yaar* (friend), you don't have to thank me" and "Come on *yaar*, no need for formality, am I not your friend?" Or even, "Shut up, okay? there is no need to thank me, no?" would have been phrases used to defuse the situation. Although there was a deep connection between us, each of us held on to our own cultural terms of expressing and receiving gratitude. **This is the point of the whole book. Friendships, relationships, and family connections are expressed culturally.**

More recently, a ten-year-old American girl asked me a provocative question: "Are you racist?" She was referring to a party to which we had invited only Indian friends. (Most Indian children would not ask this because they would be used to mostly all-Indian parties.) I found myself explaining the idea of different groups of friends, mixed groups, Indian groups, and people's comfort levels with each other. There are many Indians who socialize only with other Indians, and, perhaps even more narrowly, with only North Indians or South Indians, or even only with people who speak the same language. There are also those who have mixed groups of friends of different races, ethnicities, and nationalities. The degrees of friendship seem to be filtered by how other groups view friendship. Some questions most Indians have in mind as they assess possible friendships are: "Do they invite us back? Do they take their time to sit down and talk when they visit? Do they tolerate children and the chaos that naturally comes with them?" Depending on the answers, sometimes friendships do get categorized by race and culture.

Immigrant families from other countries may have similar values to those held by Indians, and thus the friendships thrive. It may be something as simple as how children are treated, or as complex as how children are treated. These families bring little children to a party that may last into the late hours, let them fall asleep on the couch, move them to a bed, and put them into the car still asleep. Everyone in the group is willing to put up with the discomfort of a cranky child, and no one apologizes for it. There is comfort in this, and friendship builds on comfort. A Middle Eastern family, like many Indian families, may be more willing to have heated arguments about politics and religion and still be friends in the morning. Most Indians expect that friends will tolerate intense expressions of their political and religious views without jeopardizing the friendship.

Most Indian families have two sets of friends—Indian and non-Indian—and, for various reasons, tend to keep them separate. For one, it is very easy to be with Indian friends. They may already know them from India, so the friendship goes back many years. Their parents may have known each other, and many may have gone to the same schools and known siblings and friends. They certainly have languages and culture in common, even though they may stick to English for the benefit of friends speaking different languages. The Indian friends know to come to a dinner about 45 minutes to an hour after the invited time, know how to relax and take time over dinner and talking, and are more tolerant of interruptions by family and children.

What makes these gatherings different from mixed groups is the style of entertaining, and the fundamental informality of being with a homogeneous group who probably grew up in the same city, went to similar schools, speak the same languages, and have similar parental issues and parenting philosophies. At these parties, children are almost always included, even when they go late into the night. Children's being cranky, crying, and falling asleep on friends' couches and beds is part of the accepted behavior and seen as a small price to pay for the warmth and friendship that these gatherings foster in both parents and children. The children experience the warmth of the easy friendships and hospitality of typical Indian families very personally. Most Indians see this experience as invaluable.

A friendship that begins at a workplace is not really seen as a true friendship until the person is invited home, shares a meal, and meets the rest of the family. There are expectations of give-and-take, and those who pick up on these cues enjoy deeper friendships. Indians often pay for the small meal or drink when they go out with their friends—the understanding is that there will be another time when the favor is returned and that it does not really matter if it is not. Obligations are part of the informality of friendship and strengthen relationships with the grace of accepting a small gift. For Americans who value independence and not having obligations, this Indian interpretation of real friendship is hard to understand. So, a division of friendships forms based on these exchanges. Indians tend to have and keep more friendships with other Indians, with people who have Southern (United States) sensibilities of hospitality, with those who are from European, South American, or Middle Eastern cultures, and with those who are immigrants themselves, or who have lived and traveled outside the United States. In general, in these cultures, the obligation of going to a friend's home for dinner does not end with bringing something to share such as wine, flowers, or dessert. That is just a beginning. The give-and-take is on a longer time frame—not necessarily to help with cooking or cleaning up, but to invite back within a year or so. And then the relationship will strengthen, with families inviting back and forth so that, over a period of twenty years or so, they know each other well enough. Interdependence is not a sign of weakness and independence is not a sign of strength; the relationships created form a larger social unit. Small debts and small favors owed are understood to deepen the relationship between Indian families.

Sometimes, there is confusion between cultures when there is an implied invitation to a deeper relationship. A person who is an immigrant will be disappointed when an American says, "Hey, we should get together sometime" and does not follow it up soon with an actual invitation. An American actually might have meant it at the time of expressing the offer, or just might have thought it a friendly thing to say, but a British immigrant would actually be disappointed that no specific date was set. Americans are generally viewed as too busy or unaware of having intentionality in building friendships. Many Americans are seen as incidental, accidental, or temporary friends whose friendship may end with the ending of the event or activity that brought them together. Indian immigrants definitely make room in their lives for friendships. Perhaps Americans have more family commitments (and the stereotype is that they shockingly and openly complain about these commitments) and therefore have less time to invest in building lasting friendships.

The difference could also be that Americans feel unquestioningly settled in the country, which could have many unnamed and unnameable effects of stability, ownership of country, and complacency. It seems that many more immigrants than Americans have friendships that have lasted decades. This difference in friendships may be more visible in Silicon Valley and other urban fast-paced cities than in other parts of the United States where there is a more relaxed and rooted pace of life.

But it must be noted that this is how many Indians view Americans, and that they may be missing whole sections of society by looking in from the outside. There are parts of the country that very well may have the etiquette of social engagement and friendship that is more like the Indian view of friendship. Every generalization is disproved by exceptions. I personally know many American families that have a larger worldview simply from genuine curiosity, engagement, and hospitality, and I have valued their friendship over the years.

CHAPTER TWELVE

Mixed Marriages—
The Hope that She Is At Least Indian

W hen I spoke to my aunt on the phone and told her my cousin, her nephew, was getting married, I could hear the tense silence. I let a few beats go before announcing the name, and she puffed out a sigh of relief when it was an Indian name before going on to berate me for keeping her in suspense. "I am sure she will be a good girl only, but still, Indian is Indian, isn't it?" It was only later that we discussed that even North Indians and South Indians are different from each other culturally, and how it would be really good for children to hear mother tongues spoken at home, preserve Indian culture, and continue the religious observances of their parents.

Biases and racism are a fact of life and an unfortunate truth. It may be easier to pretend that they do not exist and not to discuss their prevalence in the Indian immigrant community, but it is more important not to sugarcoat real experiences. Although negative attitudes about other cultures and communities are not the sum of my experience in the Indian community, they are nevertheless a part of it. Excluding these biases from my writing would be to leave out a truth, albeit an uncomfortable one. There is no excusing racism. Racial prejudice can elevate or idealize a group, or diminish and denigrate another group. Most Indian immigrants have stereotypic but deeply felt ideas about categorizing peoples based on their understanding of different cultures. There are broad stereotypes held within the Indian community, including cultural, color, and religious typecasts.

It is considered most preferable for an Indian American to marry another Indian American belonging to the same community and caste, and, after that, there are various categories of culture that are viewed as most complementary to Hindu Indian culture. It is an enormous shift for the whole family when an Indian marries a non-Indian. Americans, including American therapists, underestimate the importance of the change in the family system when this happens, because they do not see the view from the inside. When an Indian man marries outside the culture, the biracial couple has to negotiate the family while understanding how disappointing his wife is to the family and how angry the family is with the man for doing this to them. It is not just the parents of the man who feel the impact—the extended family is also changed in various ways by the event. It is a very big deal.

When an Indian marries a non-Indian, the families have many mixed emotions. First, they are usually relieved that their adult child is "settling down." Then there is disappointment and sadness that the family will adapt differently from the way their own families changed. The parents go through stages of grief, and mourn the loss of what might have been a more traditional family. There will be a loss of traditional values, customs, ideals, foods, language, and, most important, security for the parents of the Indian spouse. The Indian family usually worries about whether the new bride (if the son's parents are Indian) will take care of them like an Indian daughter-in-law would care for them as they age. Will the "foreign" daughter-in-law take away the social security that is their son? Will she hold the same obligations in her heart that an Indian daughter-in-law would have (assumedly) held? There are changes of expectations, dealing with disappointment, and a period of mourning before the healing can begin.

The Indian parents might actually worry that the son-in-law or daughter-in-law may not know to address them by positional names such as "aunty" and "uncle" or variations of "mother" and "father", and may instead call them by their real names. This lack of cultural awareness would grate on almost everyone and embarrass the parents. The parents may worry about how the relatives would respond. Some may be happy if "at least" she is not darker skinned, and the family can thus avoid looking into an aspect of their own self-hatred of darker complexions. On the other hand, a white person may make it easier for the family to go one step higher in the social hierarchy and can enhance their acculturation into the larger American society.

Vinita's husband died a few years before her son came out to her as gay. Her family in India doesn't know that her adult son is in a relationship that will soon include marriage to his partner. She feels uncomfortable talking about him to her more "backward" family in India, but also admits that her son did not want to talk to his father about his sexual identity. She is tired of explaining his indifference to getting married in the traditional way to family members who ask if he would be interested in meeting their friend's daughter who is so eligible. Vinita says, "I actually like my to-be son-in-law but wish that he were not of the blue-collar class. His family has not studied at all, they are all plumbers and construction people, you know." She explains that the difference between her level of education and that of the new in-laws may be too large to be crossed easily. "People in India are still not open about these things," she continues. Her main worry is not for herself so much as for her son and his partner who are very interested in visiting India soon. "We will have to be open soon," she says, because her son is in the process of adopting a child. "In some ways, it is better my son-in-law is American, for I don't have to do all the in-law things with another Indian family. Also, luckily, my daughters are all married already, so I don't have to take tension [about their being rejected because of an openly gay brother]."[3]

Some parents can be contained about their reactions; others may be very verbal and dramatic, with tears and tantrums, as they take in the information. There is usually an attempt to make the son or daughter feel guilty, as well as discussions of why they could not have picked an

---

[3] The LGBTQ movement is in its infancy in India compared to that in the United States. Most gay people are closeted, with the exceptions being in the film, artistic, and a few communities of the big cities in India. Many gay men marry women, have children, and fulfill their obligations to their families. Some of them continue to have gay relationships outside the marriage, with or without their family's knowledge. The legal system still does not support gay rights as of 2017.

Indian and made things easier for everyone. When the smoke and tears clear, if the family is able to speak calmly and be open to communicating with the new addition to the family, the parents find themselves pleasantly surprised by the ease and "non-Indianness" of the whole process of getting to know the new member of the family.

The experience of the culturally different family marrying into an Indian family can be a mix of excitement and frustration for them. There is usually the excitement of the perceived "exotic" culture, the seductive pull of Indian spices, silks, colors and festivities in the beginning, followed by frustrations with the non-stop "expectations" or cultural give-and-take of people and relatives. Westerners can experience Indian culture as very demanding and find themselves exhausted by the press of people to see, the high expectations of hospitality, and gifts to be exchanged. The stereotype of the Indian husband is that he is pampered, high-maintenance in terms of wanting home-cooked food like mother used to make, and accedes exceedingly to what his parents want him to do. He is also usually viewed as generally good-natured, devoted to family, reliable, and faithful. The stereotypical view of the Indian wife is that of a calm, practical, family-oriented, and conservative person who works hard to keep the family together above everything else.

When both families are Indian, there are understood ways of settling disputes and minor conflicts, including hierarchies of giving in and pleasing. When everyone has the same biases, there are strategic understandings of disagreement, and many Indians avoid open disagreement, choosing subtler ways of showing unhappiness. Open disagreement or refusal can be perceived as shaming, so families marrying into a non-Indian family usually have to negotiate these and other communications more carefully, as they are in uncharted territory.

The degrees of difficulty in integrating with an Indian family vary. If the person marrying the non-Indian is the only son, it can be a more difficult adjustment than if he were one of the sons in the family. More is expected of the daughter-in-law as the keeper of social norms, traditions, and family connections. If the daughter is marrying out of the culture, it may be an easier transition because the family may already have had the assumption that she was leaving the family anyway. The degree of difficulty in adjustment is also proportional to how open the family is to Westernization and how accepting they are culturally. A family with a high degree of familiarity with the Western world (a small minority) is likely to have an easier transition because they are more acculturated to Western people and lifestyles.

People from all cultures hold stereotypic but strongly believed ideas about categorizing people based on their understanding of different cultures. Deeply conservative people all over the world value things as they are now, and feel a need to resist change under new circumstances. Beneath the Indian need to stratify people as a good fit, or a not-so-good fit, is the wish for a cohesive family unit. The ideal under all these biases is the desire to continue the closeness of the family experience as it has been so far. A family with a similar immigration experience understands what it is to give up a country, to immigrate, to go through the new experience of belonging suddenly to a minority with less power, to be discriminated against, to save and be frugal, to value education as the path to becoming a member of a professional class, to work hard, to help family members with any and all problems, to keep up family and friend relationships, to be respectful of parents and take care of them, and ultimately really to understand that the family, not the individual, is the basis of all Indian views of happiness. The ideal is seen as more than just a simple respect for human dignity in welcoming a new family member. It becomes a fantastic wish to be understood completely, the assumption being that someone from your own community and sub-culture can fulfill that desire better.

Given all the stratifications of the different castes, communities, sub-communities, and states and languages in India, when the marriage is not arranged (and, therefore, from a similar community), most Indian families hope that their children will at least marry an Indian so some Indian cultural values can be passed on, allowing for more comfort in the family.

CHAPTER THIRTEEN

Whose Baby Is It, Anyway?
—Part 1

Satish and Sunitha are a young couple who are so frustrated with the school situation their son is facing that they are at the point of making drastic career changes that would be very disadvantageous to all of them in the long run. Their son is ten years old, and until recently has been a happy well-adjusted boy. He has shiny, twinkling black eyes and an engaging smile. But, as soon as he begins to talk about school, he becomes sad and hopeless, and looks towards his parents for permission to talk about it. It seems he can't do anything right in school, has only one friend, who is a girl ("And who wants a girl for a friend?" his eyebrows say), and has been sent to the school counselor for rough behavior on the playground. This referral has been the straw that finally broke the camel's back, and the parents are angry and desperate with the school system and their son, but also feel worried about having made "wrong choices for the life plan." They moved to the United States about six months ago from Malaysia, where they had lived for more than five years. On recommendations from their company executives, they had bought a home in an "A1 good school area." They are originally from India and an upper middle class environment, and are both from prosperous families that have spread out across the world. After the death of Sunitha's parents and after Satish's parents had moved to Singapore to live with his older brother, the young family decided to move to the United States. They are now "at a full stop after taking a bold step" and have to re-think all their decisions. Should they have bought into a more "Asian" school district, or should they switch to a private school, or even move back to the East? These are some of their worries as they try to figure out if their child is having a major cultural adjustment, or if the school's atmosphere is something they have to spend time understanding. Their child, who has not had school problems before, is now trying to avoid a school where he feels unsuccessful, misunderstood, and too different.

Deepa and Vish are a young couple with a five-year-old daughter and a two-year-old son. So far, they have managed to care for their children in the home with a succession of visiting relatives—first her parents, then his, then hers again, and then a cousin. Deepa and Vish are both on fast career tracks and have jobs that consume them. Deepa's sister is divorced and has regretted her decision to give up her job when her children were younger, and has counseled Deepa not to take the "mommy track." Recently, Deepa and Vish have been having many disagreements over how to manage their careers. Vish is unwilling to hire a full-time nanny who is American, and Deepa does not want the "headache" of managing help from India who may be culturally congruent with their lifestyle, but unable to drive and negotiate with the outside world, such as doctors, school, and the physical therapy appointments that their son needs. The parent generation in India is no longer able to come and help for extended periods of time. They have now decided they need more help when Deepa's job begins to require travel on a monthly basis.

Both families discussed above have various degrees of distrust of the system outside the Indian sphere of the home and family. To understand their situations more fully, it is worth looking at how differently Indians raise their children (in India as well as within an Indian home in the United States.) In the rest of this chapter, I briefly discuss the Indian worldview on childhood aspects such as infancy, transition to parenthood, the need for extra help, the duties of grandparents, where the baby sleeps, physical closeness, toys and sharing, independence, toilet training, group mothering, feeding, and transition to school.

The transition from being a couple to a family with young children is a significant one in any culture. In addition to the usual difficulties,

Indian immigrant families often have to learn different parenting styles from those they grew up with or experienced as children. Most families in India have not raised children independently as a nuclear family without extended family or other help. Most immigrant families hesitate to access childcare help from outside the family and community without quite knowing why, even if they have the economic means to get extra help.[4] This reveals the vast differences between cultures in the way that children, especially the very young, are cared for in the home.

In very traditional homes in India, the pregnant woman goes back to her maternal home after the second trimester of her pregnancy and stays there until three months after the baby is born. The husband visits her and the baby, until she is escorted back by her brother or other members of her family. Subsequent children's births are less formal for the obvious reasons of time and the demands of other children, and so the pregnant woman may or not return to her maternal home for later childbirths. Here in the United States, it is common practice in the Indian community for in-laws to visit the young family, planning to live with them for a period of six months or more, helping with the birth and the first few months of the baby's life. It is usually the woman's parents who come out to help her at this important time in her life. The soon-to-be-grandparents usually put their lives and homes on hold to help their children through what they all recognize as a special and difficult time for the new family. It is rare for a woman to go home to India to have the birth, because that would be making the citizenship process for the newborn more difficult, and the instant citizenship conferred by being born in the United States is highly valued. Parents in India consider it their duty to help each and every one of their children during this time, and go to considerable lengths to disrupt their lives in India to be of help. If they are physically unable to come to the United States, they

---

[4] This discussion pertains to middle-class families and those who are formally educated, and not the class of people in India who do physical labor. The children of physical laborers in India often grow up in neglect, travelling with their parents to job sites and amusing themselves while parents work until the children are old enough to work themselves.

usually try to find a relative who can come and help. If the pregnant woman is diabetic or has other complications in the pregnancy, even more help from the family is considered essential. The average family feels drawn in to give more help and is not intimidated by adversities encountered.

When the pregnant woman has a good relationship with her parents or in-laws, she may feel supported and cared for. When the relationship is strained, this visit compounds the stress and intrusion on the woman and the child. Many Indian families feel unable to voice their true feelings to the grandparent generation, worrying about disrupting a social process and about robbing the grandparents of the joy of the new baby's birth, all the while wondering how else to get help. The new parents are often in a state of suspension between cultures, not knowing what they want to do, not trusting their feelings, and not quite trusting the good parts of Western ideas on child care and rearing. They also feel unable to rely on getting a doula or nurse from a different culture because she may be adding yet another way of looking at things, and this may be an additional voice in an already crowded situation. They may feel temporarily able to deal with in-laws or parents even if they are "difficult," valuing their presence and help more than the peace of mind that the new mother needs. The emotional residue of this busy time can linger for decades in terms of hurt feelings and slights that went unprocessed. For example, the man may feel that his wife is too aligned with her family and that he feels left out. Or the woman may feel that her mother-in-law took more care of her son than of the new mother in her time of need.

There are unique cultural aspects to the times of pregnancy, birth, and early childhood that non-Indian therapists are usually not aware of. Questions about the birth and the immediate months after are often not addressed —for example, a separate room for a not yet separate new being. American therapists expect this to be the norm, asking questions about the baby's room that can result in the family feeling very different from the therapist, generating feelings of shame and a worry about not being understood. This is quite a foreign concept when Indian culture may encourage separation only after the child is three to five years old. But, does this foreign concept need to be accepted? Is the new mother going back to work in a few months? Is everyone in the outside world asking her if the baby is sleeping through the night? Is everyone in her cultural world asking if the baby is feeding? Who is assuming that the baby is in the parental bed? Who is assuming that the baby has a room of its own? What can the family afford in the United States vs. what they could have afforded in India? Can they trust a non-Indian caregiver whose ways are very different? Are there undercurrents of racially or culturally divided distrust between a caregiver and the new parents that cut both ways? Many of the foregoing questions are unanswered in the family and the tensions that arise from this can increase the stress of managing an already crucial time. Of course, many of these ideas and discussions can be postponed or avoided altogether if the grandparents are coming to help.

These days, childbirth has become a medical and hospital experience, with nurses and doctors substituting for the female members of the immediate family. It is still the practice in Indian hospitals not to allow the husband to be with his wife during labor and childbirth. Among immigrant families, the husband and the parent generation who have come to help are sometimes ready to be part of the birthing experience, and, in most families, the new mother is seldom left alone at the hospital. The family usually brings food that is specially prepared for the new mother, and makes sure she has all the help that she can use. Someone usually sleeps in the same room if she should need to stay overnight at the hospital. The woman's family usually provides her with at least a couple of weeks of rest after the birth. This is the level of care that most Indian families expect, having seen and experienced this level of care among their families in India. When the families are not able to match this kind of care, there is an acute sense of loss experienced by the new family. And, when this loss is added to other family stresses experienced by the couple, it can be a difficult one for the family to rebound from.

When there is a new baby in the house, most friends and relatives come to "see" the new baby—to hold it, to bless it, to put a pinch of sugar in its mouth, to bring a small silver cup to bring good luck, or to leave some money in the infant's tight little grip. A new baby is considered close to divine, having had no time to accrue any sins by wrongdoing. It is not considered intrusive to visit within days or a week of the birth, and the closer the friend or relative, the sooner they expect to, and are expected to, come to see the baby. So, receiving visitors is yet another task that grandparents help with.

In most traditional homes (where basic needs have been met), an infant (or child of almost any age) is never "allowed" to cry alone. A crying child is picked up immediately and offered the mother's breast, food, singing, rocking, and other distractions. A child shares the parent's bed until s/he is four or five years old, or is displaced by a younger sibling. Most people in India do not understand the concept of a baby's room, and view early separation of an infant from the mother as most shocking, and almost bordering on the abusive. The infant is not given any time alone—it is seen as unfriendly and abnormal that a child would be awake and alone. Physical separation is considered almost equivalent to emotional separation, and it is, of course, unthinkable in all cultures that children separate emotionally from parents at this age.

As the infant grows, there is less help, but there is a social consensus and understanding in the larger family and culture that a baby cannot be raised alone and that parenting in the United States is very different and difficult. In the upper-middle-class families in India, there may be a nanny whose sole job is to hold the baby and watch it. Physical closeness is considered important and provided by all who come in contact with the child. If an aunt does not try to reach out and ask to hold the baby, she will be perceived as strange and aloof. The regular vegetable vendor in India who brings fruits and vegetables to sell at the door will also reach out and cuddle the baby. She may also swipe at the baby's face with all her fingertips and "crack" her knuckles against her own head to remove *drishti* or *nazar*, or the evil eye's energy. Many young Indian families have extended circles of care for their children by having close relationships with Indian friends, so their children are raised with the feeling of family ties around them. The physical boundaries between children and the adults in the Indian neighborhood are very different from what is expected in the United States. Casual visitors, mailmen, and salespeople all feel free to pick up a toddler who wanders in. There is a lot of touching kids' hair, faces, and arms by neighbors, visitors, and relatives. People around the child also feel free to discipline a child by saying "no" or "don't do that" without looking for permission from the parent. This is an important difference—children raised in the United States have a bigger personal (physical and emotional) boundary around themselves.

There is less ownership of food, and sharing is encouraged. In my opinion, this sense of sharing with friends carries on into adulthood in the Indian community and is often seen in trains and public transport, where people offer to share food with their fellow travelers. Much less is expected of Indian babies in terms of caring for themselves, but more importance is placed on sharing with other children, including siblings. A very common game played with a child older than six months old, around the time when "peek-a-boo" is played, is for an adult to ask in a cajoling manner for whatever object the child is holding onto. When the child refuses, the adult pulls a pretend sad face. If the child parts with the object, although sometimes reluctantly, it is rewarded with a big smile, and the object is immediately returned with a comment of—"It is for you." Comments are made to the effect of—"She is all right, she shares, not bad!" She shares a lot!"—all praising and exclaiming about a trait that is looked for and prized. Even this little game helps the Indian child understand sharing in a very different manner than American children do. The game also teaches trust in all the adults and that it is rewarding to share. When children are at the toddler stage, they are asked to share toys and, in most homes, the toys are seen as common to all the children. Individual toys, as is common in American culture, are not the norm, but the exception. In Indian families, there might be one special toy that belongs to a child, but the expectation is that most of the toys are to be shared with other children in the household.

It is a common sight in the United States and in the Western world to see children, especially toddlers, holding onto messy-looking, much loved, and battered toys that they almost never put down. Comforting objects such as blankets and teddy bears are unheard of in India. A "blankie" or other separate object that a child physically and emotionally attaches to is rarely seen in India. When children sleep with parents, or other family members, they separate physically at a much later age, and do not use a comforting object as it is understood here. Mother's hair or clothes serve as comfort objects as the baby goes to sleep, but the idea of one particular object that is inseparable from the child (and different from just a favorite toy) is not needed, understood, or encouraged.

Toilet training among most Indian families, like teaching children to feed themselves, happens on a more relaxed schedule compared to the West. In tropical areas, hard floors are easier to clean than carpets. Now that immigrant people have to deal with the practical issues of living in the United States where most floors are carpeted, this is changing. When babies were strong enough to bounce on their feet, they were traditionally trained by being placed on the ankles of an adult while their hands were held and they were cooed at and talked to. There was no pressure to perform, but their bodies were toilet-trained at a time of day. If they wet the floor, somebody just dropped an absorbent cloth on the "accident," and the child was changed. No apologies are made to visitors who may be present. The Westernization of toilet training has resulted in the loss of some aspects of traditional toilet training. Mothers and other caregivers were aware of children's bodily functioning at a more intimate and detailed level.

Group mothering is another very common aspect of child rearing in India, with many children raised by more than one mother figure. In extended families, there are invariably aunts, grandmothers, and other relatives. In nuclear families with means, neighbors and maids are always available to a child, and it is very common for children to be raised by aunty figures who feature prominently in their lives. A mother's sister tends to be a particularly close connection, and is valued both by the mother and the culture. In fact, in most Indian languages, there are specific words for mother's younger sister, mother's older sister, father's younger sister, father's older sister (as well as specific words for different brothers). In many languages, the word for mother's sister translates loosely to "smaller mother" or "bigger mother." It seems that an acceptance of more mother figures makes it easier for Indian people to accept their in-laws more matter-of-factly and wholly, and begin to accept them, too, as some variant of "mother" and "father," even addressing them as such. In most families, the couple will come to some kind of agreement regarding how to address and refer to the parents—perhaps that one set of parents would be addressed as *mamma* and *pappa* and the other as *amma* and *appa* by both of the couple. In Hindi, the terms *daada* and *daadi* refer to the child's father's parents, and *naana* and *naani* apply to the mother's parents. In other languages, the diminutive form of the grandparent's name is added to the word for grandfather or grandmother. The adult parents never address each other's parents by first name—this is considered most disrespectful.

In many Indian immigrant families, the transition to the pre-school and kindergarten years also becomes a cultural transition. Indian parents tend to be indulgent and affectionate, viewing most childhood mischief as an acceptable part of childhood. Until about age five, children can get away with a lot. They are rarely disciplined and everything they do from whining to petulance and tantrums are understood affectionately as a child being normally childlike, and parents rarely correct the children, instead using distraction and diversion as more effective methods.

After age five, children are held accountable and taught that they cannot get everything they want, which makes for a difficult transition for most children with a lot of confusion and regression because of different expectations at home and the outside world. Fathers take on a more active role in disciplining a child at this stage. Children begin going to school and are then subject to a lot of new rules and regulations. Many children have home names and outside names. The home name is sometimes a nickname or a shortened name, but sometimes a completely different name from the given name used in documents and outside-home situations. At about age five, children are told that they will be called by their outside name at school and formally taught their outside name. They begin to understand that the outside name or formal name gets left at the door, and inside the home they have their childhood along with the home name. During kindergarten and the first few years of grade school, Indian immigrant children are often sleep-deprived compared to American children. Parents who may be late coming home from work keep their children up later in the evenings so that they can spend more time with them. Time together is a higher priority than regular sleep times, and the children often nap in the evenings after school or on the weekends. It is not unusual for the children to be up late at night, even after 10:30 or 11:00 p.m., and the chaos that goes with it is easily accepted —but sometimes at the cost of intimacy for the couple.

Eating habits are some of the most difficult habits for anyone to change. In India, it is the practice in most households for the children to be fed first. Parents and other adults usually eat later and there is less emphasis on eating together as a family, at least until the children are all in their teens or older. Even then, the cultural practice is for the mother, grandmother, or other female relative to supervise the starting of the meal and then join in. Parents often spoon or hand feed their children. This is seen as a small price to pay for ensuring that kids eat well. Mealtime is when a mother tells her children stories, often cajoling them to eat the next mouthful before continuing. The more traditional the family, the more minimal the demands placed on the child to master the environment and function independently. In families where both parents work outside the home, there can be more control issues around food. Some parents spoon feed the children until they are eight and even ten years old. Parents worry a lot more about how children eat, how much they eat, and this becomes a common fall-back topic of conversation, especially when groups of mothers get together. Added to the very Indian concept of a good mother's being one who feeds her children well, the guilt about not being available could translate into a compensatory behavior around forcing children to eat well. Even when both parents work at equally demanding jobs outside the home, the mother often becomes the "worrying-about-food parent." The idea of providing healthy, good foods for children, and letting them pick some of these and the amounts they want, is a difficult idea for most South Asian parents to understand and extremely difficult for them to practice.

There are some vast differences in childrearing practices outlined above, and a large percent of Indians feel, perhaps rightly so, that non-Indian clinicians have no idea how home lives are so different in these different cultures. This difference partly explains why South Asians do not access counseling services as much as other cultures do. They find that having to explain the lifestyle and culture is draining—when they may not quite understand themselves that there is so much of a gap between cultures—and especially stressful when they access mental health services at a time when they are already depleted. Although there is benefit in speaking about differences and therefore understanding something through a therapist's perspective, many Indians get discouraged and stop trying therapy after a few sessions.

Given some of the above differences in world-view, it is not unusual for the parents to go to great lengths to find an Indian caregiver.

In consideration of the differences in childcare discussed above, perhaps it would be easier for a clinician to see that in addition to processing grief and loss after a big move, Satish and Sunitha's son may have difficulties on the playground that get in the way of making social connections. If he comes to understand that children connect differently in the United States, and the school system encourages more verbal interaction, he may be able to translate his feelings of friendliness into a more understandable language. Instead of putting his arms around his classmate's shoulders, he may learn to invite him to come play a game at home or restrict touching to organized sports. When he understands that he comes from cultures that are very heavily biased to a lot of non-verbal interaction, he may be able to better understand that boy-culture is different in the United States, and physical interpersonal space and distance differ in various parts of the world.

Deepa and Vish may decide to consciously choose a Western caregiver that meets their child's needs for transportation and basic care, and parcel out other aspects of emotional care to an Indian caregiver or use Indian friendships for social aspects of raising their child. They could also teach a Western caregiver some of the values and principles they want to hold onto. Helping the couple sort out which Indian childcare values and traditions they want to maintain would be a part of the therapeutic work.

Holding onto Indian values of childrearing and understanding the importance of this part of parenting is like translating the visceral and primeval that one absorbs through the skin from the surrounding air into a concrete, specific, and tangible value to be passed on and taught—

much like religion or moral education. As an Indian friend remarked to me as we watched our children tumbling around, shrieking, running, and laughing late into the night, "We will pay a price for raising our children here—tomorrow, by having sleep-deprived children, and for years in ways we don't yet know. But this is what is much more important than regular sleep time." He surely meant "this" to be Indian ways of childrearing and the close relationships we look for among our friends in the United States.[5]

---

[5] In my opinion, Indian children raised in the United States (called "ABCD" or American Born Confused Desi, or fellow countryman), without a large enough Indian community to experience Indian parenting, feel a lack, and envy the stability they see in their Indian (raised in India or with a very Indian community) peers. Especially in adult work situations, ABCD Indians perversely express these feelings in a superior and condescending attitude toward immigrant Indians who have markedly Indian accents, whom the ABCD see as "Fresh off the Boat" ("FOB"). This imbalance in Indian parenting leads to a rift that is recognized by immigrant Indians, but rarely openly discussed and instead considered to be part of the American-raised Indian's personality. For example, in a software company, an all-immigrant group might discuss one of their peers as being "ABCD but friendly and open to us." Or, an Indian immigrant (aware of condescension from an ABCD) may consciously speak in an Indian accent, taking pains to show that he is just fine being higher up in the organization to an ABCD who may work for him and that he does not feel inferior to the other just by dint of accent and upbringing. (ABCD and FOB are discussed in more detail in Chapter Nine.)

CHAPTER FOURTEEN

Whose Baby Is It, Anyway?
—Part 2[6]

In the Indian expatriate community, there is a cultural phenomenon—prolonged early separation between a child and the parents and the Indian community's participation in this occurrence — that is significant, sad and troubling. This separation—spanning a period of a few months to a few years—often begins about the time the child is weaned or a year old and involves entrusting the child to the care of grandparents and extended family (usually the parents of the mother) while the mother tries to establish a more stable home and work environment (often in the United States.) This chapter is the longest one in the book, and its length is a reflection of the intensity of grief, loss of culture, and family disruption that is a big part of immigration and other similar separations that occur in the community.[7]

This separation phenomenon, which rarely existed forty to fifty years ago, is best understood within the cultural context it occurs so that it can be appreciated in its complex entirety. It is culturally condoned but inherently traumatic (in my opinion) for all—mother, father, child, and

---

[6] An excerpt of this chapter was published as an opinion piece in the San Jose Mercury News on February 20, 2011.

[7] The understanding of this phenomenon may be extrapolated to some other cultures that participate in this kind of separation, such as some Asian, South Asian, Middle Eastern, and Mexican immigrant families.

grandparents. The families attempt to deny, minimize, or blind themselves to the effects of the separation, perhaps because it is too painful to consider fully and consciously. Some of the rationale behind these separations is easy to understand, and some is not. It is important to consider the underlying factors that go into this emotionally wrenching experience for all concerned.

A child is born into a family web that is interlaced with ideas, beliefs, values, and feelings that are shaped by cultural pressures, family heritage, and personally held truths—some of which mesh together and some of which do not. In recent times, globalization, fast transportation, and technology have helped shrink the world. As people have made accommodations and used the world differently from their grandparents' generations, they have overcome hurdles of distance in order to achieve education, financial stability, or other less tangible (but still important) gains. Some of the accommodations run counter to some very deeply held basic beliefs. Moving far from aging parents is one of these. Another is the more unthinkable act of giving up of a young child by the mother, no matter how temporarily.

To have a son in the Indian culture is to have everything.[8] Yet, it is more often that a son is temporarily given up than a daughter. Since separating from a child is not something undertaken lightly, what forces come into play in the decision to leave the first-born child with grandparents? Often the parents are convinced that this separation will give them time and energy to develop and mature their educations and careers. For others, the separation may allow the mother to develop her mind and/or her identity, but the expressed reason is always financial need and improvement. In still other families, the separation may mean that the father will have more uninterrupted access to his wife and thereby help her to achieve more earning power. More often than not, it seems that the mother makes this decision to create for herself what is not offered readily by the culture—a separate identity of her own, something more than motherhood. In making this decision, the mother has to wrestle with a clash of cultural, and sometimes personal, values.

---

[8] See Chapter Seventeen for a description of male privilege.

I have witnessed first-hand from parents their experience of immense guilt, remorse, and pain in this separation, possibly one that compounds the previous separation that happened with immigration and the subsequent breakdown in the maintenance of a multi-generational family group. In a culture that does not hold with early physical separation and individuation, this early separation is mysterious, troubling, fraught with guilt, and is sure to have echoes in the family's emotional life.

The effects of such a break span many years and perhaps even generations. I have noticed that a mother who undergoes this separation in her childhood is more risk-averse in the family's later life. She tends to view minor temporary separations that occur naturally in a growing child's life somewhat differently from mothers who have not experienced extended separations, encouraging the child to stay close. In my observation, she is more likely to let the guilt from the early separation influence her family life and "hover" over her children more than others. I have seen mothers often numbing themselves to the grief of that first early separation by discounting it, distancing themselves emotionally, and normalizing such separations. The family behaves outwardly as if nothing abnormal has happened, especially since the separation is not considered taboo. This kind of separation is, sadly, not unusual in the Indian immigrant community now, and almost all families have heard of some relative or other who has sent a child "home" to be raised temporarily by grandparents.

I find that there are echoes and reverberations of the separation in the child's later life. An adult who was sent "back home" as a child may determine that a separation of that nature will not recur between her and her offspring. The child who was left may become a very "good" model child. Such a child may live with a profound deadened and dissociated split-off part of the self that haunts, and not know where that feeling of loss came from. Or, the sent-away child becomes a very anxious parent experiencing breakdowns and disruptions of functioning. Some may become over-protective parents or even repeat the separation in their children's lives. The experience of being left behind often becomes a part of the core identity of the person who was separated from parents while being raised by grandparents.

This separation is different from one that occurred in times of war when children were sent to the countryside for safekeeping. It is also distinctly different from another kind of separation in which young children aged four and above were sent to either a boarding school for a "better" culturally appropriate and more consistent education, or entrusted to a relative so that they could have access to better schools.[9]

The manifest reasons quoted by parents for temporary separations are different from the less obvious reasons. The rationale often provided is: time to finish a course of study to be better equipped for a job; time to work and get established in a job or new country; time to take care of problems in the marital relationship; or, most important, lack of adequate caring help. The parents minimize—but do not usually deny—the pain, grief, and hardship they endure during the course of this break. However, they often deny any effects, or are unwilling to speculate about the effects, of this separation on their children—the grief, pain, and disruption in their very continuity of being. In fact the parents often represent the separation as a net positive for the child—the children get to grow up with Indian values, experiencing the love of the extended family, all before they are old enough to really miss their parents. These children, as young as a year or less, are not yet able to experience or comprehend that they are separate beings from their closest parent. Those parents who are able to look back at the separation after many years are most often regretful that they allowed it to happen, wistful for the lost time, as well as puzzled that they did not have the wherewithal to have found a different solution at the time.

---

[9] The wartime and education-centric separations have their own ramifications, some of which may not be different. These experiences are not discussed in this chapter. The British presence in India may have made this sort of separation easier to accept because the British families stationed in India often did send their children away to be educated in boarding schools in their homeland — in a more accepted and culturally similar way to their own. The children who were separated from their parents during wartimes had cohorts similar to their own and it was clear that the separations were to give them better chances of survival and were more easily understood as essential. It would also be interesting to delve a little deeper into the subject of these separations to see if the parents who give up their children temporarily have shadows in their family of wartime separations among the parent and grandparent generation.

During the actual time of the separation, the parents are stoic about the fact, grieving the separation, but also viewing it as necessary in the face of an absence of alternative choices. Whether they seriously considered and discarded available daycare as less trustworthy than family care is not always clear. Some of the women were very emphatic that they considered caring for their child a full-time occupation, were sure that they could not provide it at the time, and found the best substitute—a mother or mother-in-law. Some women talk about how their mother (child's grandmother) asked for the child to be left with them, and how that was a factor in the decision-making. Still others cite it as the most practical (but simplistic) way to have their child experience a traditional upbringing closest to their own, while also benefitting from the loving care of grandparents. Most of the women I talked to about this felt quite certain they would have to give up their careers at least in the short term if they did not send the child away.

The fathers fell into one of two categories—either passively deferring to the wife's decision or actively suggesting that the child be cared for by the older generation. I did not hear of any fathers who voiced an opinion about that choice being the wrong one for the child and family. I have also not had an opportunity to interview families who considered and rejected the choice.

I will use the term *"repaired families"* to refer to these children and their families once they were reunited. According to *Merriam Webster's* online dictionary, the transitive verb "repair" means to restore by replacing, or putting together what is torn, or to compensate for. According to a general understanding of the word, if you repair something that is damaged, you do something to make it right. When you repair an object, you restore it to a good or better condition. The word "repair" is also commonly used for setting something right or addressing a wrong. Repairing something gives vitality back to it. The word's various uses evoke the many feeling states experienced in these families who come together after a separation. The families are re-paired with feelings often unrecognized consciously, but feel surges of energy towards relationships and broken feelings that need attention. Unless the family clearly recognizes the newness of what was generated by splitting the family, they blind themselves in limited and destructive ways, and fail to recognize that the *repaired* family is very different from the original family. Determined atonement often prevails in the families described—the mother often tries to make up for the break in the family's existence by holding the child or herself extra close in many ways. The term "*repaired*" families fits the people I describe for all meanings of the term.

As a therapist, I have found that migration—in these cases, to the United States—is in itself a traumatic event, whether chosen by the individual as an act of moving from motherland to a foreign land, or secondarily experienced because one's parents migrated. The migration often echoes and magnifies previously experienced family separations. In these repaired families, the first separation is the transition from an extended family in India to a nuclear family. The second separation is from a mother in the United States to a grandmother in India. And the third separation is from grandmother in India back to a mother in the United States. Another possible separation could have occurred in the grandmother's younger years, if children (either her generation or her children's) were sent away for safekeeping during times of war. Each separation compounds the strain of the previous one. It has taken two or three generations and separations to fully produce the psychological dilemmas and accumulated historical and familial issues that lead to the experience of *repaired* families.

The foreign land becomes a fatherland, a place that is conceived of in terms of separateness for both parts of families that are far away from each other. The motherland and emotional landscape is left behind. The fatherland later also becomes a land of re-unions where the parents have more opportunities for education and work. The fatherland can be viewed as a developmental stage that comes after the motherland in the emotional life of the child. When a child is separated too soon from the mother, it is almost as if milestones and developmental stages are not fully experienced but skipped over. It is like a child's running before going through crawling, then tottering, and then walking. When a developmental stage is skipped, the later stages may have less substance and foundation to them. The movement to the world outside the mother is substituted for by a chaotic back-and-forth that may leave the child bewildered about what relatedness really feels like, and can cause the child to not really "get" relatedness because s/he has lacked the ordinary gradual transition to the world outside the mother. Secure relatedness needs to be felt in the bones, deep inside, and not from a thinking and separate place outside. The repaired families did not think about this clearly when they chose separation. They perhaps could not. In fact, they more than likely did not comprehend the enormity of what they were embarking on, for understanding it clearly would make the separation almost impossible to carry out.

When multiple mothering in an extended-family situation is not just part of cultural awareness and familiarity but an expectation, the idea of raising a child "all alone" can be a daunting prospect. When combined with a move to another place—either within the country or out of it—added to the expectation that the mother of the child also work or study outside the home—raising a child becomes even more complex and challenging. The world outside the home seems—or is—more foreign, and the family doubts, distrusts, and fears the childcare associated with the larger foreign culture. In these situations, the model of the extended family's providing extra help and parenting lowers the barrier to giving up a child temporarily to the grandparent. Leaving the child with a trusted grandparent is seen as a short-term practical step that eventually benefits the whole family. The family views the idea of the child's being cared for by extended family members as a completely natural form of childrearing. It may not feel qualitatively different from what the mother had experienced for herself. It is just many, many, miles away and does not factor in the emotional needs of the child for the physical presence and feelings of connectedness with the child's parents that would occur daily.

It is an accepted norm within South Asian cultures that physical closeness between parents and young children is different from that in Western cultures. This is manifest in the idea of the "family bed" as well as in a commonly held view that a child sleeping alone in a separate bed in a separate room is someone to feel sorry for. So, when the child is sent to be with grandparents in India, the understanding is that there will be physical closeness with the grandparents in terms of living and sleeping arrangements. The physical closeness will be with the grandparents and not the parents for the duration of the separation. The grandparents are understood as exchangeable and the mother *in situ.*

However, the child's experience is one of repeated loss—first of a parent or parents in a move far away to extended family that often includes grandparents; and then, second, of grandparents when returning to a new home with parents that is foreign in people, place, smells, and sounds. The child re-experiences the ruptures of the parents' immigration process, but collapsed into childhood, without the benefit of being an adult with a discriminating mind. That a child has a complex emotional life is something regularly denied by the Indian culture, which emotionally permits parents to move children around without imagining what that would be like for them. When the parents have not understood, processed, and grieved the trauma of the migration and breakup of the larger family, how can the child? The parents have been traumatized themselves, and most cannot bear the pain of confronting this trauma. This blind spot—that often comes with the experience of trauma—makes it easier for the parents to send the child away temporarily. It is easier for parents to feel pity for their child's sleeping alone in a room, but not for their child halfway around the world, because s/he will be held physically close by the parents' immediate family. Although the parents carefully consider the physical wellbeing of their child, they do not similarly consider their child's emotional life.

Trauma is more readily understood and accepted if it is a discrete event in a shorter time span than if it is a longer period of unacceptable untimely separation that is painful for the child and the parents. The separated child often has a stronger desire to please the parents, even during their teenage years, and is less tolerant of parental strife compared to the child who experiences no separation. This separated child does not rebel and assert individuality in typical teenage ways of partying, staying out late, or using drugs and alcohol. Instead, s/he achieves and stays close, often physically and emotionally. In my understanding, these separated children exhibit more anxious versions of dependency than is the norm for the culture, and take a much longer time to establish their own separate emotional lives, often waiting until they are adults and can merge with an intimate partner or spouse.

Karuna walks heavily and has a vertical worry line in between her brows that makes her look as if she is frowning all the time. She scratches at her head, sighs a lot, and digs around in her purse to find the prescription for an anti-anxiety medication that a doctor has written for her. She tells me that work stress is too much, that she is sleepy at work, and that "Kannan, my husband, is asking too much, wants this and that all the time, can't see at all, and ayyo, appah, too much. I am going mad only." Kannan looks defeated, shuffles his feet on the carpet, and says, "She is like this all the time. I am telling her to take the tablet, no? But I can't earn more, or telling her to go home and I will come after two years. But no, all the time she is telling paining, paining." When I ask if there has been recent weight gain, she says she has actually lost weight and it is now ten months after the baby. This is the first mention of a child and I find I am shocked, and wondering if I heard clearly. It turns out that the baby has been left behind in India with her in-laws, but they speak to the in-laws almost daily. Karuna continues, "They are telling, Ammah [mother], baby is not crying, but baby should be crying only, just like me." [Ayyo is a Tamil expression of loss, shock, or distress and is variously used to show worry. Appah means father, but, as with Ammah, is also used to swear disbelief if spoken emphatically.]

In another family that is more chic and urbanized, the father and mother come from two different states in India, and have different mother tongues. They have Hindi and English in common, and also a child sent to India to be cared for. Hema is from a North Indian state and Hindi is close to a mother tongue for her. Sridhar is from South India and his parents do not speak Hindi. They come to me to discuss the huge conflicts that Hema has with her in-laws. Hema says, "The tipping point occurred because Anup now talks Malayalam only! Arre! [Exclamation in Hindi, which means anything from a hello to an angry response]. I can't speak it, they did it purposely only!" Sridhar says sagely, "So what? He will learn quickly to speak in English and children learn languages really fast anyway." This statement inflames Hema even more. Hema's mother died before she got married, but Hema now feels "my mother's death is with me everyday when **my** son can't speak to me in **my** language." She is outraged that their child has to relearn his mother tongue. She swears she will never let him speak Malayalam again and is suspicious of her in-laws almost to the point of paranoia.

With yet another family that has separation at the root of their functioning, the family flounders and is unable to understand the significance of some of the events in their life. Savithri wants to leave her husband and take one of her two children with her to start life anew in Singapore. Her husband Shiva wants to hold the family together, but is at a loss to understand her, especially when she says she has found another older man, wants to leave her husband for him, and "his whole family loves me, but my in-laws are forever fighting with me." Savithri herself was raised by a grandmother and then "reclaimed by my mother when the time was right." Savithri accuses Shiva of being a "baby and a man-child who has not grown up, who watches TV, and does gaming all the time." Shiva is the only son of doting parents who had five daughters before him and consider him the final blessing on their lives. Shiva and Savithri sent their firstborn back to India to be raised by grandparents to "get past the difficult early years." And now, Savithri wants to take "my younger happy child who is not clinging and whiny all the time" with her to Singapore where, according to her, "life is not so chaotic and there is plenty of household help." Moreover, she thinks her new family will have closer access to caring adults "who can all together help with the child." She says Shiva expects too much from her and she finds him young and too dependent on his parents. But she is unwilling to examine her immature behavior in wanting to jettison part of her life and one of her children (who has already been impacted at least once by an untimely separation) so that she can be better cared for by a new and exciting family. "They will be like me, I was also taken by grandparents, and I am okay, no? It will all be fine in the end."

These three families have another cultural value that is common to them—they are more traditionally Indian in their thinking and other norms. They are more likely to have, and be completely comfortable with, only Indian friends and family. They are less Westernized in their thoughts, beliefs, and ideas. When one is less trusting of the outside world, there is often more difficulty acculturating. The American world that is part of their everyday working world is literally left at the door, along with their shoes, creating a clear boundary line between the two cultural worlds. The inside of the house is more Indian in its décor, positioning of art, and the practicality of the home. The living room is often converted to a family play area that later morphs into a common study area. There is more likely to be a "family bed"—one or more beds that the whole family shares and that is used by all the children and adults in the home, often until the children are six or seven years old or older. There may be some suspicion of the world outside the front door that would raise questions like: Would there be beef (taboo to religious Hindus) in the food? Will the nanny drug the child? Will the outside world be less "clean," and more polluted by touch, habits, or other differences? Often, the culture and world outside is experienced as something external that is very slowly absorbed, that can't be ingested yet, and can't be held too close, creating a self-imposed segregation from the Western culture into which the family is relocated.

The mother of a separated child uses denial, self-deception, and sometimes dissociation to keep from fully feeling the depth of the grief she experiences. The father is quieter and almost shame-faced as he faces his impotence in the matter. He feels financial responsibility for the state of matters but usually does not permit himself to show that he is emotionally moved. They are often stoic as a couple and adopt that style of functioning for the duration of the separation with the almost complicit understanding of, "What to do? We had no choice—it was too difficult." Despite the fact that this separation is condoned among many families, the women all wanted me to understand that it was, in fact, not okay. Even if it was done "all the time," it was not all right.

While the Indian culture supports interchangeable mothering figures as part of the multiple-mothering model, long separations are not part of the equation. Immigration is, in a sense, another long separation—from family, country and culture. Broken intra-family ties, especially with children, even though temporary, are smaller but more powerful repetitions of the same separation as immigration. In working with South Asian immigrant families, I think it is important to be aware of the possibility that parenting figures other than the mother and father may have raised the child. The parenting figures may have included aunts, uncles, relatives, nannies, or grandparents. Additionally, the parents may have been absent for a length of time, the child may have been twice separated from close parenting figures, and most important, the patient may not consciously recognize this as something significant.

The self-protective denial mechanisms are convenient, in that they allow the couple to develop the dreams and ambitions of the mother. In coming to terms with the fairly new notion that the mother's work and cerebral life are as important as the father's, the couple feels unable to take on the challenges of caring for a firstborn without the family system that was in place "back home." The childcare facilities that exist in the community seem outside their zone of comfort. The father finds himself emotionally and idealistically unable to step in and provide an unfamiliar level of support to the mother. And so the couple leaves the baby with the grandparents. The young family rationalizes their decision by equating the "mother-infant tie" "with mothering figures-infant tie." It is unbearable to look at the reality of what reuniting truly is—almost an adoption of a barely verbal child back with the mother in a foreign place after returning from an adoptive grandmother and family.

I feel very strongly about this kind of separation—that it should be avoided if at all possible. And if this chapter could in any way help to end the practice or to get families to stop and think clearly about what they are about to do, I will have done my bit towards ending something that is truly distressing to all involved.

CHAPTER FIFTEEN

Born Again—Born Free, Living Free, or Forever Free?[10]

Reincarnation is the belief that the soul, upon the physical death of the body that contained it, is reborn or embodied in another physical body. Reincarnation is a fundamental concept in Hinduism and is widely accepted among Indian people. It is interesting and important to know how this belief system is woven into the fabric of everyday life of many Indian people.

Reincarnation is not viewed as an end-of-life concept that is of importance to only older people. It is a rich, pulsing, and very much part-of-life vein that weaves through everyday life. An American friend who visited India told me she was no longer the same person she was before her visit. She said her visit and experiences there fundamentally changed her. This is a common experience to many people who visit India, even those who have traveled widely and seen the different ways of life of people all over the world. The difference is attributed to a spiritual quality that is part of the very fabric of life in India—the corner shrines, the symbols of religiosity in buses and cars, the incense in the air, and the mixing of all of this with the humdrum reality of poverty, plenty, and the bustle of everyday life. Others besides this friend have commented on how they saw, were

---

[10] These are titles of three books by Joy Adamson popular in India: *Born Free* (1960), *Living Free* (1961), *Forever Free* (1962). They tell the story of a lion cub that was adopted and then sent back out into the natural world.

115

astounded by, and changed by the very visceral quality of experiencing other people's lives being lived out in front of them. People who have lived and grown up in India have learned to shut this down so that they can function in spite of the extreme stimulation all around them. But those who go in from a quiet aseptic world are often stunned, over-whelmed, and changed.

Another friend told me he had to rethink his belief that poor people were unhappy. That had been his assumption until he saw poor people in India having many happy moments and interactions that included laughter, friendship, sharing, and a sense of interconnectedness that made grinding poverty and hunger more tolerable. Their sense that their lives were not just this body in this time and space made for more lightness of being. Accepting your lot in this lifetime may be easier if you believe that your present life is a result of how you lived your previous one and how you live this one will dictate your next life.

In my practice, I see this belief reflected in a woman who tells me that her life is not happy, but it is not too unhappy either. She was not living an ideal life with an ideal partner, but she had decided that, in this lifetime, there was only one marriage for her and she would accept her difficulties. Her neighbor, however, struggles mightily with her life, but, then, perhaps (according to my client,) that was the neighbor's lesson in life—to struggle and face unhappiness when there was so much going right in her life. She said that if she were her neighbor, she would know that it was not good for her to struggle so much—she should accept her life in this body and then do good so that she would have a better life in the next round. This belief in the "next round" gives her a stoicism and a non-solipsistic way of viewing the world and her place in it. This feeling and quality of being no less than another or no more than another may have been what my friends were trying to give words to. The beggar children playing in the street stop their playing to go and beg for food, and then go back to their games with their friends. They don't seem to think about how the child in the car is so lucky and they are so unfortu-nate, but that the child in the car has other challenges than food and shelter. Seeing and experiencing things like this changed my friends—they saw spirituality and religion on every corner and not segregated into a church and temple, and they saw a quality of connectedness and hope that transcended everyday grime and life.

"She is her very grandmother incarnate—I can see it in her eyes and her stance," says an aunt to her sister-in-law about their niece. The niece's grandmother had died a few months before she was born, and it was commonly held that she may have her grandmother's soul. It was not made much of but not hidden from her either. This family had some formally educated people with careers in medicine and law, and they certainly knew enough about genetics and inherited traits. This did not, however, keep them from talking about and believing in souls that transmigrated, and the belief also gave them some comfort when they grieved for the much-loved grandmother who had died. "She loves us and has come back to give us happiness," was one of the comments. They gave this niece a name that was a modernization and abbreviation of her grandmother's, and, in doing so, they held the grandmother close in their hearts.

A recent Bollywood movie is another example of how reincarnation and the belief in it is a part of life in India. The movie told almost two separate stories, connected by a death and a birth. The heroine in the first half is in love with the hero, and a villain thwarts their love. In the second part, the heroine is reborn into another body after the villain kills her, and she gets revenge on the same villain although the injustice was done to her in a previous lifetime. The movie was billed and viewed as a love story where karma plays a part and not advertised or understood as a story about reincarnation. The reincarnation aspect was casual, accepted, and just a small oh-by-the-way portion of the story.

There are Western therapists and New Age gurus who help people discover their past lives and look into them to help with situations in their clients' (present) lives. This is too concrete by Indian standards, and is a Western imagining and Westernization of a Hindu belief. It is a subtle difference, but an important one. In the Hindu worldview, rebirth is an unquestioned aspect of being alive. It is something that is so intrinsic to the culture that it is unquestioned. Progress, and the changes in society it generates are unquestioned in the West and expected at an almost visceral level. It is understood commonly in the West that, with each generation, life gets better, and this is so firmly accepted that to question it would be almost heresy. Almost no one I know in India would even consider wanting to look into their past life to make sense of their present one. You live your current life to your best, and the cards you are dealt may be based on how you lived your previous lives. How you live now will determine your next. This unquestioning belief in karmic inheritance is a core value that helps many Indian people lead a more contented life. It also helps people live a more "free" life, knowing that somehow there is only so much struggling can accomplish. A person who struggles and fights life a lot would elicit comments about the certainty of more lifetimes and rebirths. The ultimate goal across many lifetimes is, of course, in the direction of *moksha*, when the soul is forever free from rebirth.

As part of understanding an Indian person or client, the discussion may never come around to the belief about reincarnation because it is primarily a personal and sometimes unexplored aspect of the self. The belief or nonbelief in reincarnation is as hard to question as a belief in a god and religion. Some Hindus have traditional beliefs about gods and have a favorite deity that they can relate to. They usually pray to the usual spectrum of deities. Other Hindus have a strong personal belief in a godman or saintly mother figure and seek out blessings and advice from them. But both kinds of Hindus will consider rebirth a part of their belief system. It is a fundamental belief, and even more private and personal a belief than any other aspect of Hindu religion. Most people in India, or even the immigrant formally educated population in the United States, would find it hard to deny the existence of reincarnation and would prefer to treat it as something that is unknowable. Most Indian people would acknowledge that there is more to life, people, and phenomena like astrology and past lives, than science and our limited senses can know—divination of many types is an essential part of the culture. A person is never born free—one is always born into an inter-connected world of families and peoples. A person lives in freedom by being clear that there is only so much that can be controlled and changed. One works to be free of life and its impediments, all the while trying to be dutiful and free of the cycle of birth and rebirth, even while knowing that it is a struggle to get free of the previous lifetime's Karmic debt. By striving through lifetimes, perhaps a person can escape the cycle and then become forever free—*Nirvana.*

CHAPTER SIXTEEN

Dharma, Karma, and the Cycle of Life

At three years of age, my nephew had already absorbed some of the ways that most Indians understand death. When the family pet died, he asked why another soul could not come into the body and bring his cat back to life. We had no answer for him except to say that the body was tired and the soul would go free or come back in another body in another place. We would miss the cat, but the cat would also always live in our minds, and be near us in other ways. We would always feel the cat's love for us but we had to let go of the cat's body. That is how the family consoled my young nephew. Death is understood differently in Hindu culture and is quite different from the way that most Western societies consider it. Death is viewed as a comma, or a semicolon, and not as a full stop.

To extend the example of the cat, the family might have also talked to the child about what a good life the cat had led, that he had done his duty (perhaps in the killing of mice), and that he would no doubt be born into a higher life or even never be reborn and thus achieve Nirvana, or relief from being tested in various earthly lives. People in the family might have enviously looked at the cat napping in the sunshine and commented that they would want to be reborn as a cat in a good household, and be pampered and loved until death. It would have been normal for the child to hear comments such as these.

The goal of human life, according to Hinduism, is to live a life that will free you from the cycle of rebirth. The soul should be set free and not be reborn in another body. The life you are in is considered the fruit of your previous lives, and is accepted as "fate." Your lived life is your *Karma*. It is your destiny as defined by the actions in your previous life, but is also shaped by your actions in this life. When you live a good life filled with *Dharma*, or duty to your family and yourself, as best as you can, it sets the course of your life in this lifetime as well as in the next. *Dharma* is your duty as defined culturally, ethically, and familially. Death is seen as the next step in the soul's evolution, and people who have tried to live a dutiful life are rewarded with a better life in the next incarnation. The ultimate goal is for the soul to be set free of earthly links and never be reborn.

When these understandings of *Dharma*, *Karma* and *Moksha* are taken seriously by the culture, it adds more depth to the significance of horoscopes and astrology in one's everyday life. The common belief is that almost everything is preordained. There is an implicit understanding that somewhere out there, there exists knowledge about what is going to occur in your life. Someone with other-worldly connections and "sight" into a life that is not visible to all, may be able to give you a view of what to expect in your life. A good astrologer may be able to get glimpses into broad areas of what is going to happen in your life. A seer in a room filled with stacks of palm leaf inscriptions can pull one out which will tell you if your son, whom you are so worried about, will ever get married and have children. This kind of belief system does not mean that people will not pray for changes in their life. Prayers and promises of vow fulfillment to various gods are seen as part of your struggles in accepting your life.

A family struggling with a young mother who is dying of a malignant cancer will consult and get treatment from Western medical doctors but also offer various prayers and consult astrologers. An astrologer will usually not predict things such as death but instead say things like, "It is a very difficult time for the family for the next few years." Or, the astrologer may say, "The child has more than one mother figure." A family priest may prescribe some prayer rituals to help the family grieve after the death. A garlanded picture of the person may hang in a prominent place in the home. *Kumkum,* or the red powder or paste that most

Hindu women wear on their foreheads between the eyebrows, is often put on the photograph. These are ways that a family grieves and keeps the person in their midst. When the grieving is complete, family members will say things like—"She left us," "His soul left me forever," "We have to wait for the next life now," or "Her purpose in this lifetime was over."

Most Hindu homes in India have a sealed container of water from the holy river Ganges. It is, of course, stored in the *puja* room where prayers are offered and idols and pictures of gods reside. Either a separate room or a dedicated space exists in almost all Hindu homes and is the heart of the family. When a family member is dying, the seal is broken open and a few drops are poured into the mouth of the dying person. This serves to wash away some of the sins accrued in this lifetime and help with a better rebirth for the soul of the person.

The last rites performed are supposed to help the soul escape from the body. As soon as it is washed, dressed, and decorated with flowers, the body is cremated. For ten days, no food is prepared in the home where the death occurred. The whole home and all the people in it are considered to be in a state of extreme pollution. This state of pollution can be best understood as almost being in quarantine. Visitors to the house who come to console the grieving family would observe the rituals that go with the cleansing of pollution, like showering and washing from head to toe when they leave the house where the death has occurred. On the tenth or thirteenth day, all the favorite foods of the dead person are cooked, with friends and relatives joining in the feast. The ten days are filled with ritual, prayer, offerings to gods, and there are prescribed practices that encompass the family. The funeral pyre is to be lit by the son. If there is no son in the family, a son-in-law or close younger male relative does the duty. The son's role is not only that of provider of material and everyday care for aging parents, but also of provider of children and the continuance of the family. Most important, the son also helps release the soul of the parent from this lifetime. He is also bound to offer yearly prayers on death anniversaries for the wellbeing of his parents' souls. Some families observe death anniversaries of their parents for five to ten years. Others may observe a day of ritual prayer, donation of food as alms to the needy, or a simplified ritual for their lifetime, or as long as they are able. Some explicitly ask their sons to do the rituals for only 5 years; or even tell them to do no ritual after the first year so that their children do not feel burdened.

While there is discussion of several worlds in Hindu myths, there is no concept of Original Sin or heaven and hell as eternal reward and punishment. Hell could be thought of as being reincarnated as a person or animal in a miserable life. That would be your *Karma* for wrongs you do in this life. In addition to this belief system, there can also be a belief in a temporary good place and bad place where you may go after you die.

A man might remark, "It is *naraka* ahead for me. I am committing the eternal *paavam* of not taking care of my mother in her old age." *Paavam* is Tamil for "a remarkable bad deed or neglect of duty that carries over as bad Karma into your next life." The opposite is *punyam*, which is Tamil for "a good deed that is above and beyond ordinary deeds, giving you a better Karmic inheritance by adding merit to your next life." *Naraka* is a temporary netherworld where one will have to serve time for small or big sins after which one would be reborn or sent to *svarga*, or a heavenly place.

In India, it is completely normal and not contradictory to hold two opposing or contradictory views at the same time. A child was born into a family in my neighborhood within a year of the grandmother's death, and was given the name of her grandmother. Many relatives remarked that she was a lot like her grandmother and it was easy for people to believe that the grandmother was reincarnated as the new baby. As she grew up, there were even more obvious comparisons. At the same time, the parents continued to observe the yearly ceremonies for the wellbeing of the soul after the grandmother's death. There is no discomfort with the irrationality of ceremonies when the soul is already in the home in the child's body. If questioned about it, the family members might say, "Why not do ceremonies? It is for the best anyway. We don't really know what happens. So, why not do some good and get *Punyam*?"

Dharma also encompasses other aspects of a well-lived life, such as living a good life that is balanced and not overly indulgent. Most families have an understanding of what it means to have a good life. It is the *dharma* for parents or the eldest son to help educate and settle (as in a job and/or marriage) the children, a part of *dharma* to grow up and support parents, to get married and have children who become part of the larger family, to invite family members to religious occasions where you feed them and be a good host, to visit family and have them visit you, and to have a balance of pleasure and work. That is part of their *dharma*. Most people take that very seriously and feel guilt and sadness when they neglect any part of it.

One of the two great Indian epics is *The Mahabharata*. *The Mahabharata* describes the conflicts and battles between two sets of cousins. A part of *The Mahabharata*, the *Bhagawad Gita*, or the Song of God, forms one of the most important sources of Hindu philosophy. The *Bhagawad Gita* is the conversation between the god Krishna and the warrior Arjuna, who is one of the Pandava brothers. Krishna reminds Arjuna that his duty should come first and that, even though he does not want to fight and kill his cousins, it is his *dharma* to his family and his subjects to fight the war, doing his best to win it. Doing one's duty gets one the highest merit, even if it involves killing.

In *The Mahabharata*, the story of *Yudhisthtira* and his ascent to heaven is also part of the Hindu understanding of *Dharma*. *Yudhisthtira*, the firstborn and eldest brother of the warrior *Arjuna*, was the son of *Dharma* (or *Yama*, the God of Death), known for his adherence to truth and rightful living. After the war was won, and after years of ruling the kingdom rightfully, he and his family give up their belongings and make the journey to heaven. The other family members' bodies fail them because they were loaded with remnants of wrongs from this lifetime, but the son of *Dharma* almost reaches heaven. He is asked to leave his dog behind, so he refuses heaven, saying he would not abandon his loyal companion. The gods are pleased by his answer, for the question was another test, and it is revealed that the dog was *Yama* in disguise. He is further tested when he is shown into a heavenly place, which he refuses when he hears the rest of his family is in a hell, preferring hell to a heaven without his family. This parable of duty and family is an inspiration to do one's duty even in the face of death and what follows.

All these rich myths, stories, history, and parables make it fairly easy for people raised in Indian culture and symbolism to accept nuances, uncertainties, and have more tolerance for difficulties in life, including the acceptance of death. There is more of awareness that people close to us do not really die but live within and among us and, therefore, stay close to us. In my opinion, there is more of an unconscious and rich primary quality to this way of thinking. There can be an overlap between the idea of rebirth and the ordinary idea that people don't really die but are alive in our minds. It is qualitatively different from the Western more logical and secondary way of rational thinking alone, where a person is either dead or alive. The Hindu way of accepting death is closer, in my opinion, to the unconscious, where several contradictory things can still be true, making for a more delicate, nuanced, and multifaceted acceptance of death that lives among all of us.

CHAPTER SEVENTEEN

Male Privilege and Its Price

As the oldest of grandchildren on my mother's side of the family and the oldest of children in our immediate extended family, my place as a girl child was unquestioned and secure. Until I was about ten or twelve years old, I was almost unaware of the absolute ultimate importance of a male child. That was when I had made a new friend who had just returned to India after living in the United States for many years. The experience of introducing her family to mine jolted me out of my complacency and opened my eyes to the world's view on the importance of gender.

In particular, I was excited to introduce my friend and her mother to my aunt. My aunt smiled and observed the common courtesies of welcoming them into our home, asking them to sit down and if they would like something to drink. My friend's mother said she was busy and had to go soon, and so they had a brief conversation at the door. Looking back in time and culture, I realize now how that small interaction itself was different—a new acquaintance would not refuse the offer to come in and sit down. It would be seen as unfriendly and in poor taste to not sit down for at least a few minutes. My aunt then asked her mother about the rest of her family. In response to the question of how many other children she had, my friend's mother replied that she had another daughter younger than my friend, to which my aunt's response was, "Oh, that is all? Only two girls?" "Yes, just two," said my friend's

127

mother. And the conversation did not move onto other topics. My aunt continued, "No boys?" "No other children—just my two wonderful daughters," said my friend's mother. It was at this point that I perked up and began to take notice of the back and forth. It might have been that my friend's mother's posture had shifted, she may have crossed her arms, and her voice changed and became lower and slower as she said that. My aunt picked up some discomfort and said something to defuse the atmosphere and may have even laughed at the "wonderful daughters" for it is not an accepted thing to say something like "wonderful daughters" or make positive comments about children in front of the children. But the point had been made—two daughters were not enough because there was a lack of a male child.

Looking back, it was clear that my friend's mother had encountered such questions before and had found a culturally different way of pushing back. An "all-Indian" woman may have said something different— such as, "What to do, it is what it is" or "This is what God gave me." My friend's mother had experienced a different culture in the United States during the 1960's, where women had new power even if the United States did not pay women equal pay for equal work or have women leaders. She was also one of many daughters in a family that was very educated and egalitarian. She was speaking up for daughters everywhere and for parents who had to face this brutal question, which implied, and rightly (for the culture) too, that a lack of a son was a very difficult thing—whom would the mother live with in her old age but a son, because a daughter would be living in her husband's family. I felt the tension, and it changed my path and opened my eyes. It made me wonder if there had been disappointment at the time of my birth, and if my parents would have had more children if the next child had not been male.

The above incident happened in the 1970's, and things are different today in India—at least in some social and economic circles. Recently, in 2014, two children of a maidservant[11] died in a tragic accident, leaving

---

[11] Termed "domestic help" in a socially different world that may cringe at the old terms, maid and servant are still accepted usage in India.

her two other children who survived. As she grieves about her immense loss, it is clear that her loss is more tragic to her because both of her boys died. One of the surviving girls said to me that she should have died, so her mother would have at least one boy and one girl. She was giving voice to her mother's— and the culture's—view that her life was less valuable than her brother's.

The significance of a male child is a vast topic that has a huge impact on the cultural, social, emotional, financial, and afterlives of South Asians. According to Hindu religious belief, the eldest son has to light the funeral pyre of his parents and perform all the religious ceremonies that release a person's soul from the body after death. Ultimately, a son releases and is responsible for the souls of *all* his forefathers. In his parents' lifetime, he and his wife bear the responsibility for their health, care, and welfare. According to Hindu Undivided Family law, the eldest son is usually the inheritor of the family wealth and responsibilities after the death of his father. If he has younger siblings, including unmarried sisters, his responsibilities include their education and getting them married and settled. In a family with no sons, it is often arranged so that one daughter marries a man who is one of many sons in his family, and the bride's family then informally adopts him to be their heir and the one who can perform their death rites.

There are many myths of the male child as god. *Krishna*, the incarnation of *Vishnu*, the preserver god, is worshipped all over India. He is worshipped as the baby *Krishna*, as the young adult who satisfies many women, and as the philosopher God who delivers the sermon of the *Bhagawad Gita* to a doubtful warrior and reminds him of duty without looking for the fruits of rightful action. Many of these stories and myths are woven into the fabric of everyday life in India, as well as into people's psyches. There are several rhymes and songs for little children that involve *Krishna*—"*Krishna, Rama, Govinda ...*" —but they are almost all built around a male child. For a religion that has a vast number of goddesses who are powerful figures, the lack of playful girl-child myths is puzzling but also understandable. While the birth of a male child is celebrated, the birth of a female child is downplayed at best and mourned at worst in many parts of India. Gender selection against females and female infanticide have led to unequal gender ratios in many parts of India. On the other hand, every household would like to have at least one daughter named *Lakshmi* after the goddess of wealth. In large part, this attitude of worrying over too many girl children is because the girl child is viewed as eventually belonging to another family—to be "given away" along with a dowry and an elaborate wedding (a financial hardship in many families). Her husband's family becomes her new family and, in some communities, she will rarely visit her maternal home again. Some families speak openly about not getting too attached to their daughters, as something to guard against so that they can avoid a painful loss later. Some daughters, in turn, respond to this rejection with a bitterness that seldom heals.

In families where there are several girls, and the long awaited son is the youngest, the aching yearning for a male child frequently has as an unfortunate outcome—a downright spoiled son who is smothered and mothered by his mother and several older sisters, often making him a very entitled and narcissistic person, causing grief and ruined relationships for the whole family, including himself. There seems to be a formula to create this kind of young man and families are usually aware of the rights and burdens of marrying into a family with an "only son." The wife of this man will have a lot of privilege but also the responsibilities of caring for his parents and pleasing his sisters, who can either make her life a lot easier or much more difficult.

Over the last fifty years, there have been many changes in the Indian family structure caused by better education for women. As more women have entered the work force in middle class families, their earning capacity is part of the decision-making in the number of children the couple plans to have. Many families decide to have only one child so that they can invest more time and money in the child and also so that the mother need take less time away from work and the money it brings in. This decision has forced several changes in society, including the changing roles of the only girl child who also takes on the role of the only boy. Young women are quite aware of their responsibilities to their parents and include this in their decisions when they get married.

Mamta is twenty-eight years old, an engineer by training, practical and no-nonsense, and looking to get married. She is looking for a partner who is also an engineer so that they can help each other in their work lives too. She is interested in traveling and seeing the world before settling down somewhere near her parents. She is the only child to her parents and acutely aware that her parents are her responsibility. She has decided that it is important to find a man who would understand her situation, and help her care for her parents. In return, she is willing to care for his parents, too, but has rejected many suitable matches in whom the man is the only son or the eldest son. She views them as having too much to do already, and is upbeat but determined, even when her parents tell her to not worry about them.

Mamta is an example of a young woman who is confident and can verbalize that she has a financial and caretaking responsibility to her parents. She may marry into a family that has more than one son, so that the duties of taking care of the parents can be split and therefore more manageable. As an only child, Mamta has been far-thinking enough to consider that she may have to play the role of a son someday. This might require her to participate in the cremation rites of her parents, something usually barred to women.

Even when both siblings are equally well-educated and employed, a brother can feel extreme stress when his sister has big problems in her marriage. He feels compelled to help her, to talk to her often, and to support her—all while sometimes taking his own family and health for granted. On the flip side of this, when young couples fight, the young man may pick up the phone and call his in-laws or his brother-in-law to complain about the behavior of his wife and to ask for their help. Adult sibling relationships are more complex than in Western family relationships, and trouble in them can have a serious impact upon the mental health of the family. The immigrant population tends to underscore this commitment by adding the responsibility of being in a larger community (away from home) without the support of an extended family. So, staying connected becomes even more important. Children are often told specifically that they have to take care of each other, and the falling-out of adult siblings causes extreme heartache to the parents and the whole family. Even after a family has been in the United States for more than two or three generations, it is common to hear comments about how "the children do not have more than each other—after all we live here and not there." The grieving for a lost community and the feelings of loss of physical and emotional connectedness takes a very long time to heal. Staying connected to traditional cooking and art forms is a way to stave off the intense feelings of loss of homeland, so much so that the immigrant families are often more in touch with traditional art forms compared to their kin in India.

In a traditional Indian family, the first male child is never expected to leave home to establish his own home. His emotional reliance on his mother is slowly transformed into a responsibility to take care of her. In general, there is an assumption that the girl will leave home and that the boy will not. This gets built into many interactions and expectations. For example, it may be that the parents will have a joint bank account with the son and have a separate bank account for the daughter with the expectation that the son can put money into that account as his parents get older so that he can support them. The family may be more comfortable asking for financial support from the son if there are urgent medical expenses, and may not ask the daughter because of the underlying assumption that her income may be dedicated to her husband's family. The oldest son may also have unspecified expectations of him—he may be the one that the parents will live with as they age. A change in this order usually creates some disharmony.

Until a few years ago, most adult Indian males living on their own were considered (especially by the older generation) unable to function without women. They were viewed as "poor things" because they had to cook, clean, and launder for themselves, especially when they moved out of the country. Since little was expected of men in terms of self-care, most of them were not taught these basic skills, as the assumption was that the mother would do these things for them until the wife took over. So, adult males who move to the United States often had no idea of how to cook, clean, or fend for themselves, and learned these skills with other men like themselves. They often look for and room with other Indian men, treating each other as a form of family.

Indian men are privileged in a very special and different way than elsewhere in the world. In the Western world, men are privileged and this is rationalized by the idea of carrying on the family name through male children. Among Indians, this privilege is more nuanced and complex, while also still integral to the Indian family system. It is linked to the responsibility of taking care of elders. Men are proud to admit that they turned down a good job offer from a prestigious company or stayed in the country so that they could continue to care for their elders, even if their wives or additional help did most of the actual work. Conversely, if a man is unable to provide for his parents it can be a source of much shame. A friend told me that he was now free to do what he wants—he had taken good care of his mother until her death. It was a matter of great personal satisfaction to him and he counted it among the better decisions in his life. He chose to stay in India and personally care for her and walked away from, almost certainly, more money. The family might also have valued living in India, doing good for the country, as well as ideas of not wanting to be a "second-class citizen" in another part of the world where "you have to prove you are good enough." Other families that value adventure, starting afresh in a land of more opportunities and an easier life, make the decision to leave older members behind at least temporarily. The "green card" of legal permanent residency that is so highly valued in India comes at a cost that is not always easily obvious.

At some level, the parent generation of immigrants has "permitted" them to leave, trading their own "social security" so that their children can have better lives. The immigrant generation carries a heavy burden of guilt of not being physically available as parents get older, and of being unable to take care of parents who are ill or aging. Added to this is the actual cost of sending money or material gifts home. Immigrant men feel this burden more intensely and feel huge internal conflict if their wives do not have a good relationship with their (the men's) parents, and this gets in the way of caring for his parents. This generation of aging parents who bless their children's choice of moving to live in another country underestimate the difficulties of aging far away without the physical and emotional support of their children.

Namitha is about forty-five years old and part of the "sandwich" generation. She takes care of her family in the United States including her son and daughter, but also feels responsible for helping her parents in India. Her brother has chosen a non-traditional route of traveling the world on his own as a photographer and writer, choosing to be fulfilled in his life while ignoring the duties he was raised to be aware of. On every visit "home," she tries to guide her parents on problems she sees them dealing with—problems that would not exist if her brother had been more dutiful (by marrying and having a family) and had found a way to live near them. She realizes that the extended family of cousins and grandnephews and nieces help her parents out, and feels much obliged to them, but also has to deal with barbed comments about neglect of duty. She sees no way out and returns from each trip to India with a heavy heart. She is sure her brother has a more difficult time of it, but he has chosen to focus on his life and is not available to her or her parents in an emotionally supportive way. She tells me she has chosen the only way out—she pretends that, in her heart, her brother is actually a "sister" of whom social expectations would be different, and that her "sister-brother" is disabled. This creative tactic works for her, but not her parents or extended family who feel shame, anger, and irritation that they have an able male who does not do his dharma. They cannot ignore his being. She tells me it feels similar to how one might experience a seemingly able-bodied panhandler and wonder why he was there at the side of the street asking for handouts instead of working.

At thirty-five years of age, Omkar feels he is too young to have high blood pressure and headaches, but these symptoms take him to the doctor who rules out organic causes and advises that he learn to deal with emotional stress. After some work with a therapist, Omkar decides he and his wife have some work to do together. Problems between his parents and his wife have come to a head and he has avoided talking with or visiting his parents for more than five years. He recently heard from cousins that his father was ill. The shame of having to hear from cousins who obviously know that something was wrong between them, the guilt of not doing his duty, and the dread of being overwhelmed with feelings when he actually sees his parents have morphed into acute physical stress.

Somaticizing mental stress is one of the acceptable ways for Indian men to express emotional pain. It is commonplace to go to the doctor and complain of not feeling well, be diagnosed with high blood pressure or digestive problems, to actually fall down, and then find ways to talk about stress in the family. A man may talk about disquiet in the emotional brain or stress in the physical brain caused by work. A family doctor is respected and expected to be able to help with the physical and the emotional aspects of stress. Many immigrant families look for an Indian doctor who can understand them culturally, and keep the relationship with the doctor similar to one they would have had in India.

While keeping the above facts, stories, and myths in mind, the therapeutic community may help Indian families more comprehensively by understanding male gender roles, the hierarchy between genders, cultural mores, and how they all play out in everyday life. Some gender roles have changed in the last forty or fifty years—and some have not. The commonly understood stereotype of an Indian man (with a disclaimer that this is a caricature even within the Indian community) is that he is a good provider who is unduly influenced and emotionally controlled by his mother; who is emotionally immature with his wife; who is frustrating to care for because he feels cared for with complex time-consuming Indian food like his mother made him; who wants to be the head of the household and very concerned with respect shown him; who will care for his sister more than his wife; who will protect his parents with his life; who wants only the best grades from his children; who deems emotional matters inferior to rational ones; and who can be easily manipulated by women. Like all caricatures, there is some truth in it, for typical Indian parents raise their sons very differently from how they raise their daughters. Indian male privilege has its price in terms of physical and emotional health, guilt, and difficult relationships.

CHAPTER EIGHTEEN

Repetition, Ritual, and Redoing

OCD is one of those annoyingly overused acronyms that in common-speak becomes nothing more than a determined personality trait, as in, "I am really OCD about it and try to make sure I get all "A"s." Given the general awareness of at least a hint of what the acronym means—Obsessive Compulsive Disorder—one would expect that people would also get help when these sorts of behaviors become problematic.

Compulsive behavior is an attempt to manage and control obsessive thoughts that won't go away and are persistent enough to be problematic. Some people are unable to get rid of intrusive thoughts and find it almost impossible to turn their energy away from it and towards constructive and essential work. They experience high degrees of anxiety until they can manage to tear themselves away and often come up with ritualistic ways to manage the anxiety.

Based on my experience with the Indian population, there appears to be a higher prevalence of Obsessive Compulsive Disorder in the Indian community when compared to the larger population. Regardless of the actual rates of incidence, many Indians commonly deny the existence of a problem when it borders on the "psychiatric" or has anything to do with the mind. In spite of more recent medical understanding about how the mind and body cannot be separated into two distinct and separate spheres, the Indian community prefers the label to be more related to the body. In some ways, there is a feeling of unavoidability when it comes to somatic problems and no personal responsibility or shame associated with it. A problem with an emotional or organic basis that is connected to the mind is seen as a frailty, a failing, and a fault. A diagnosis of such a problem is usually wrestled with, and not accepted until it is extreme and undeniable. The need to deny it comes at a high cost to the person and the family—emotionally and socially. And, paradoxically, it eventually affects one's peace of mind, which is highly valued by most Indians.

Kumar and Latha have an in-law problem. Latha's parents are visiting and they both agree that her mother is a very difficult person to have around the house. But recently, Kumar has stopped talking to his mother-in-law, and, according to Latha, "The situation is full tense and I am talking for all." Their adolescent son refuses to talk to his grandmother too. The parents have come to help Latha's cousin who is about to have a baby, but it seems as if they need more care than they can give. Latha's father cooks for everyone, having discovered his talent recently, and the idea was that he would take care of Latha's household so that she could help the cousin whose parents have died recently. It now seems as if Latha's mother needs more help herself. She has been put on some mysterious medication that she won't discuss. Most troubling is the fact that she washes the sinks and bathroom down everyday, and sometimes more than twice a day. She washes it in the way it would be washed if it were a bathroom in a tropical country where everything is made of concrete and tile. She does not accept that bathrooms in the United States are not designed to be hosed down like the sidewalk. Latha has managed to keep her out of the kitchen so far, but suspects that her father has taken on cooking to protect the family from the fact that her mother is unable to do so anymore. He has hinted that she gets stuck on the washing and does not progress further in the cooking process.

In further discussing their family, it turns out that they are extremely worried about their son. He is about to enter high school and Latha and Kumar are at odds about the decision. Latha complains that her son is a perfectionist and is very particular about his grades. He has never got anything less than an A+. She wants him to go to the less demanding school, saying that she knows how stressed he gets when he has a heavy academic load. Kumar wants him to go to the more competitive school because that will "increase his chance at the Ivies." Kumar proudly describes his son as, "a very, very neat, clean boy whose room is always spick and span," and that they cannot enter his room even to put his laundry back. Latha says their younger child has started to tease her brother about his hand washing routine. It takes him a full five minutes to wash before dinner, and Kumar predicts a surgeon in the family. When I ask them to consider a pattern in their family of cleanliness taken too far, the couple say that they "don't want to consider anything 'psychiatric,'" and decide that just telling their kid to stop washing should be enough.

When formally educated Indian families are unable to access care because there is such shame in needing psychological help, the suggestion for appropriate help needs to be made very cautiously so that they can be more open to hearing and accepting it. When there is so much shame around disorders of the mind, it has sad results—people don't get the help they need.

Latha's mother is in a kind of agony. Nobody wants to think that they fail psychologically, but this is even more so in our immigrant Indian community. There is such a need to deny the truth in the situation that it is remarkable that the family even got so far in getting my help. Latha is to be admired for even getting to this point in help-seeking. She sees that her mother has few to no choices and is almost nonfunctional. Narcissistic feelings of shame do not prevent her from trying to get appropriate care. Kumar, however, was not ready to confront the evidence, and I was unable to prevent their flight from psychotherapy. There was a high price for this denial—the helpless in the family are the children, and they suffer their shame until the community and family can wake up to reality. As Latha said, "I give up, I can't do this all alone, no? I need family with me." In giving up, she also gave up on getting appropriate help for her child, and although the family pressures are understandable, it is likely that their son will have difficulties later on in his life. There is no magic wand, and treatment would require patience, kindness, and perseverance.

Deepak's family avoids most social occasions that involve food. The family is held hostage by Deepak who does not trust that any food made outside the home is clean enough for them. Given that most Indian (and other) social situations involve food's being shared, it is difficult for the family to go out and make friends in the community. Deepak's wife complains that all her time is spent managing the situation at home. If a cooking utensil were to fall on the kitchen floor, it is thrown away as washing it would not do to make it usable again. Sheets are disposed of after visitors leave, and laundering is not an option. According to his wife, he shouts at their child when she touches her nose or face, and has her immediately wash her hands and face. When there is an inability to tolerate the usual clutter and chaos of a home with children, there is a loss of connection with the real world and a narrowing of perspective. To many people, that should be a clue that all is not well and that additional help is needed, but Deepak denies a problem and refuses to consider treatment.

The San Francisco Bay Area and Silicon Valley attract a lot of technology workers who are skilled in mathematics and other subjects that are precision-oriented and perfectionist—something either works or it does not. This population of workers is understood to have higher rates of Asperger's Disorder and other Autism Spectrum Disorders. Perhaps OCD prevalence is correlated to this population.[12] It is also possible that OCD is easily masked and passes unnoticed in India. A culture that has many daily rituals around prayer and the preparation, cleaning, serving, and consuming of food can easily camouflage this disorder. Some communities have very set standards of hygiene rituals, and, at this time, I am speculating that there may be some correlation or genetic inheritance of the disorder in the population. The lifestyle in the United States may make obsessive traits more obvious and not part of the ground. It should be easier for Indians living in the United States to ask for psychological help, but the fear and shame connected with anything in the psychological realm are not much different from that of the Indian population in India.

---

[12] I have not had the opportunity to verify if my informal observations (and those of a few colleagues) regarding the higher incidence of OCD in the Indian population is indeed true. That information is beyond the scope of my work and this book.

Many Indian people avoid the word "cancer" even when there is a clear diagnosis. They prefer to use the more neutral word "tumor" because refusing the label makes a life-threatening disease more manageable and perhaps less lethal. The difference is that they do seek treatment for diseases that are clearly, to them, somatic. There needs to be a tipping point at which the family seeks help for deeper psychological problems that take over and impact every aspect of life. For psychological problems, there may not be a clear tipping point, but it is better to err on the side of earlier intervention. We cannot experience the richness of life if our minds are more absorbed in the management of a piece of the home. This is like looking at a crack in the window frame when there is a bountiful and expansive view outside the window. When the pain of packing for a vacation becomes so intense that one would rather forgo the vacation, quality of life is at risk, and forgoing treatment is not only irrational but also detrimental and painful to the children raised in such an environment. I am encouraged that the younger generations are open to getting help, as changes in the media and popular films begin to depict varieties of help-seeking.

CHAPTER NINETEEN

Rules of Engagement

K*uchela's* story is of universal relevance. It is the story of old
friends, their friendship, and the impact of life's changes. The
god *Krishna* spent his boyhood among the humble *Gopis*, or
the cowherds, raised among them as one of their own. When, in time, he
conquers his evil uncle *Kamsa* and regains the throne that is rightfully
his, he becomes a god-king, living in splendour and among nobility. His
childhood friend *Kuchela* comes to see him, fearing embarrassment,
wondering if his old friend will even recognize him after all the years.
Krishna greets him with joy and humility, washing his feet for him, and
making him sit next to him. He then turns mischievous and quizzes his
friend, asking what gifts he has brought. *Kuchela* hesitantly offers him
the humblest of gifts, an offering of pounded, preserved, and dried rice
prepared in the way that *Krishna* used to enjoy as a boy. *Krishna* eats it
with great relish and much greedy enjoyment, putting his old friend at
ease. *Kuchela*, a man of learning and devotion, "forgets" to ask *Krishna*
for help with money to feed his children, but when he goes back home,
he sees that filling *Krishna's* stomach has merited him and his family a
life of ease and freedom from poverty.

There are many lessons from this story, but the one that holds importance in this chapter is the grace with which *Krishna* puts his old
friend *Kuchela* at ease, valuing his humble gift and protecting him from
shame. Most Indian Hindus are raised with such stories of the value of

old relationships and the importance of keeping in touch with old friends.

Tarun is trying to figure out what he did wrong. Although he has retired from the world of high technology, he still keeps busy serving on advisory boards, including a local school board, investing in angel fund groups, meeting young people in start-up companies, and providing free consulting for them. He has made his money, his children are settled, and he is enjoying an easier pace of life. He speaks with some anger and sadness about a recent encounter with a former protégé. Years ago, Tarun had given Shiva his first job out of college, recognizing in Shiva a passion and an enthusiasm for the field. Shiva did well, and the two went on to different companies. Shiva kept in touch, and so did Tarun. When Shiva had losses in his family life, Tarun paid his respects. Over the last two years, Shiva stopped returning Tarun's messages. Recently, Tarun has heard that Shiva has moved into his neighborhood. Tarun saw Shiva at his local coffee shop one morning and found himself walking away to avoid a face-to-face meeting. He now talks of being sad, but also angry. He cannot decide if he was saving Shiva face or protecting himself from more sadness by walking away. Tarun knows he wants nothing from Shiva—neither thanks nor indebtedness—for there is no debt. He wants just an acknowledgment of an old relationship, which may in itself be the gift.

Janaki describes herself as "somewhat Aspy" (short for Asperger's Disorder), a gifted musician and mathematician, a generous person, and a steadfast friend. She has a steady group of friends who all belong to the same music school. She talks about a sense of camaraderie in this group. In addition to weekly lessons, they enjoy meeting in one another's homes every month to practice and share dinner. Another group that she is loosely associated with, however, she finds more troubling. This group is made up of the families who send their children to the same religious school, which teaches the children the basics of Hinduism, mixing in some morality and lessons in Indian culture. It draws its members from the three or four surrounding cities, and the children have met every Sunday morning for years, and a few friendships have developed among some of the families. She feels that, for some reason, she is "not getting some basics" in this group. She feels ignored and sidelined and can deal with it, but feels badly for her daughter who is feeling the pinch more. She does not know if it is "my own Aspy naïveté," or if there is something bigger that she does not understand. If it is a life lesson, she wants to be sure to pass it on to her daughter. Apparently, of the four cities that the school draws from, some cities are higher in "snob value" than others. She has felt snubbed by a couple of the families who live in the cities that have higher home prices and has felt judged by the value of the car she drives. She says she and her husband prioritize education and believe in living a modest life. She does not advertise the fact that their house is paid off, that they own other properties, and that they send their daughter to private school, but is re-thinking some of these values when she sees that her daughter is not invited to some parties and trips (like ski weekends) where there is the expectation of being able to afford a certain lifestyle. She says she hates herself for thinking like this, but is wondering if she is being too naïve. Given that a lot of their close friends are Indian, she feels quite dispirited about the classist attitudes, but also wonders if she should help her daughter deal with some of the rejection. "Why not see if this person is kind, intelligent, and decent, instead of how big is their house, or what car do they drive?" she says.

Racism exists in numerous forms and many Indians can talk about incidents of racial prejudice they have experienced. A woman talked about her experience of being politely smiled at in a polling station on Election Day and then being ignored. The people at the very upscale neighborhood polling station had assumed she was "just" the nanny. Another woman said the officer who pulled her over for a traffic violation was condescending to her, assuming she was a babysitter, and that his attitude to her changed as soon as he figured out her address was a multi-million-dollar mansion. These are a few examples of prejudice about skin color, and these kinds of prejudicial things do happen in everyday life. Most Indians also say that Americans in general are the most accepting and generous people they meet, and that these instances of racial prejudice are far outnumbered by the thousands of normal and pleasant interactions among most of the community.

Classism and prejudice within the Indian community *vis à vis* the classism in the rest of the world is more nuanced and layered. There are unstated but powerful rules of engagement that are in play most of the time. There is a shared belief in a system of hierarchy where people need to know where the other fits in. There is a very significant expectation of respecting the bonds of obligation. There are also unstated rules of making sure the more powerful protects the less powerful from feeling shame. When these unstated rules are violated, there can be a lot of dissonance in the family structures and sometimes people do not know how to grieve these losses. Sometimes, these rules are as simple as money and position and sometimes more complex, as in in-law and family interactions. These questions can be essential to solving the obstruction in the family system—"who is shamed and who is protecting whom from shame?"

The awkward encounter that Tarun is wondering about reflects the loss of a previously close relationship between him and Shiva. He can't account for the cooling-off of the relationship. He wonders if he might have offended Shiva in any way, or if perhaps he neglected him somehow. He checks to see what his wife may have heard and finds she knows nothing more than that Shiva's parents have come to live with him while his wife is away in India taking care of some family situation. That by itself would not be very significant, but Tarun is no wiser as to why Shiva has been avoiding him. A few months later, Tarun's wife hears that Shiva's wife actually was living separately and locally. This makes a little more sense to Tarun, and he feels relief that perhaps there is an explanation after all. Shiva may just be embarrassed. Shiva may wonder what Tarun knows, if he should tell him about some of the problems he is facing, or he may just not know how to talk about family and respond when Tarun asks about family and how everyone is. Tarun feels more comfortable knowing that he just needs to normalize things with Shiva and invite him over to a café to have a cup of tea, keeping conversation to work areas. After that, it would be up to Shiva to keep up the relationship or not.

Janaki decides that the time is ripe for sharing more of her values with her daughter. She discusses culture and class, prejudice, and judging people by their outward appearance, as well as trying to look for the good in people. As she talks to her daughter about different kinds of prejudice, she is pleased to hear that her daughter has found a sub-group that is more interested in the kinds of activities that she likes. They find a way to talk openly about the snobby girls and families, but decide to invite everyone to a summer party and then see if anyone would be interested in renting a house together for a long weekend's ski trip. Janaki's daughter is also able to talk to her mother about how clothes are very important in a teenage girl's life, and convinces her mother that a little peer pressure about fashion may do them both some good. They decide to go on some fun fashion shopping sprees, and Janaki allows that, "Yes, my dress sense is not too good—I am quite basic." It is a different kind of pressure but it may be one that can afford them some mother-daughter fun in the process of fitting in a little more. They decide they will not compromise their values too much but that they would give some of the families another chance and keep their sense of humor in being "Boston Brahmins" in California!

When children are growing into their teenage years they try on different personalities as they find their own sense of individuality. When Indians move to the United States and cannot find an easy way to stratify, their own backgrounds and the families they come from don't have significance anymore. They go through their own version of adolescence until the next generations can rest more securely in their identity as Indo-Americans. Perhaps being insecure in identity, using money as the marker, and being snobbish are part of the growing pains that the culture is experiencing.[13]

---

[13] The Bay area now has a large enough Indian population that it can be easily subdivided based on mother tongue. There are now Tamil, Telugu, Kannada, and Malayalam groups for people from the four Southern states of India, and groups from Maharashtra, Rajasthan, Uttar Pradesh, and other Northern states. Most people from the Northern states have a basic familiarity with Hindi, although Bollywood has had the unexpected but unifying side effect that most young people raised in India can now speak Hindi.

CHAPTER TWENTY

Mind the Gap!

The atmosphere was tense and the hall was packed. Necks strained to look up at the podium where there was no one yet. I was in a sea of black-haired heads with a few lighter-haired heads scattered here and there. Everyone looked focused and anxious, as if they were afraid they might miss an important announcement. I was at a high school information night. This particular school attracted many from the South Asian and Asian[14] populations because of its reputation of focusing narrowly on a high standard of academics and structured learning. The word "because" in the sentence above is in itself telling—it is an accepted stereotype that Asians are more interested in a higher level of academic achievement.

Another high-school open house I attended had a more casual feel. There was chatting and laughter and a feeling of lightness. Going by just hair color, it appeared to be a more diverse group of people. It was clear that the staff was trying to manage an event and show their school in the best light, but the buzz in the air was qualitatively different. It seemed as if the teachers and staff were there to meet and talk with the parents and students in a relaxed setting. Everything was just a little more casual.

The differences above could be attributed to just two different kinds

---

[14] In this chapter especially, "Asian" or "Indian" refers to people from those areas who are the immigrant generation or who are the first one or two generations.

of college prep schools—if the demographics at the school events were not so startlingly different. The first kind of school caters to and is composed of an almost exclusively Asian population. The second type of school draws from a more mixed population. When the majority— 75 to 90%, and not just 35 to 40%—is from any one social or cultural group, the school does begin to cater to that larger population. By "cater," I mean not just to be overly accommodating and clearly trying to please that group, but almost swept up and carried away by the value systems of that larger group.

The staff and faculty of the first Asian-majority school came from diverse populations— a very small fraction of the staff and faculty were Asian or South Asian—and seemed motivated and accomplished. It is clear that the students at this sort of institution accomplish more in terms of extracurricular activities and are highly successful academically, reflected in the large number of admissions to Ivy or other "difficult to get into" schools, the median GPA, and the college admission test scores. One of my concerns is that these children may "burn out" earlier than other populations. I have anecdotal evidence from my practice as well as from my colleagues that these children struggle with the intense pressure they face from the ultra-competitive school systems they belong to. These school districts focus narrowly on Science, Technology, Engineering, and Mathematics, succumbing to pressure from parents to get rid of the more "light" classes in Humanities and Arts. These children are known to be more vulnerable to higher rates of stress-related illnesses and have elevated rates of self-harming behavior and suicide attempts.

Rina, an athletic, vivacious young woman who is a senior in a local high school comes to see me after a suicide attempt. She says she did not mean to kill herself but did not know what to do with her anger and sadness. "I am never enough. I am never going to be enough. They will never let me live down my one "B"—there is nothing I can do anymore that will make them happy. I can see his eyes stop at the B on my transcript, and he has looked at it so many times!—I can't bear it anymore." Rina had come home drunk and fought with her mother. She is ashamed that she can't fight with her father openly. Rina had admission into a good school, but it was not high enough on her father's list of top schools, so he had taken to avoiding parties on the weekends where there would inevitably be discussions of schools the children got into. In a drunken anger and after a fight with her mother, he had told Rina he wished he did not have children. That was when Rina overdosed on painkillers. The parents also refuse to come in to meet with me at her request, as they are worried that someone might find out that they visited my office.

The above situation is an example of one high achieving family pressuring their child to follow in their footsteps. There are many other children who do not crack under the pressure, but who keep it all in and wait until they get out of the home and into college, before they realize that they cannot enjoy life. Another concern is that this emphasis encourages a formulaic approach to checking off boxes to attain other boxes to check off. While the formula seems to be working at one level, in that it is seen as a pipeline to high-paying jobs, it does not seem to make those children feel confident and secure. My worry is that it leads to a population of disconnected and unaware children who go through the motions expected of them. If the end goal of the extreme academic pressure is a high-paying job after attending a prestigious college, the pipeline does work. Personal satisfaction, inner strength, and happiness are not the stated goals, or, perhaps are secondary goals.

In the great divide between "white" parents and Asian parents, each maintains strong stereotypes of the other. An Asian perception of "white" parents is that they are more interested in the social aspect of their children's lives, about their friendships and dating, or about the sports their children are involved in. This is looked down upon by most immigrant Asian parents who "know" that the best schools lead to the best colleges and then to the best jobs, and, thus, to the security of having enough along with having the envy and respect of their peers. Asian parents do not understand why "white" parents are not more worried about their children's high school academic achievement, and why they don't push their kids more.

On the other hand, most "white" parents feel that Asian parents are too pushy and game the system while not respecting that their children are individuals who should have freedom and choice in high school. When the population in any town grows over time to be more than a third Asian and South Asian, changes happen in the system. There is a proliferation of eating, working, and studying establishments that cater to the Asian community. More tutoring study centers spring up so that children can be even better prepared for school. Many children go to Friday and weekend school to learn not only their native language but also for extra preparation in math and writing. A Western mindset would call this extra schooling that is robbing childhood. An Eastern perspective would be to think of children as needing to be kept busy so they don't have too much idle time to get into trouble. It takes a couple of generations for this mindset to change. The Asian immigrant generation feels pressure to get into the higher educated class as quickly as possible. The immigrant child who grew up with such pressures often turns into a parent who is more "white" and refuses to put her/his own child through the same wringer that s/he experienced. Or, these people still keep a very high level of expectation, but feel they are not so demanding as their parents were.

But when a town changes too quickly, there are feelings between different communities that clash with each other. The town may not be prepared for immigrants to come in at a higher economic level and make changes in the system. In the past, the pattern of immigration was usually that immigrants came in at the lowest level of society, did the physical labor and jobs that most "Americans" didn't want, and slowly got acculturated over generations. This is a different time in the immigration history of the United States, where immigrants who look clearly different are coming into the middle to upper classes and making changes in the culture and community through the schools. On a family level, these changes may be felt acutely in a clear "us vs. them" mind-set.

When Ganesh and Hima come in to see me, they are angry and withdrawn from each other after repeated and heated arguments about the best choice of school for their child. Their daughter Indu is fourteen and very likely to be accepted into four different private high schools. Their fallback choice of their local public school is also "not a bad one." It is highly ranked and in a prestigious school district. They have discussions every night about the best choice for her. These usually end with Indu going into her room and quietly closing the door. A friend's mother calls Hima and says she is concerned about Indu. Indu has confided in her friend that she hates her life and has been hanging out in inappropriate chat rooms, even giving her cell phone number to people she has met in these electronic forums. Hima is shocked to see explicit text messages between Indu and total strangers. Indu has also said she no longer wants to play volleyball, which used to be something she looked forward to every day.

Ganesh is an accountant in an investment company and Hima spends her time being a homemaker, keeping the home beautifully decorated, meeting friends for coffee every day, working out to keep fit, cooking, shopping, keeping in touch with relatives in India, and volunteering at an Indian charity. She is well-groomed, confident-looking, and the bag she carries is smart and trendy. Ganesh looks well put together, too, but there is a softer air about him—he looks more relaxed after he runs his hands through his hair. He looks at Hima and says "She takes care of everything for us, all things, and Indu must listen to her. But we must also hear Indu. She is after all American and not all Indian like us."

Hima discusses how much she does for the family. Everything is done by the time her husband and child come home—dinner is cooked, everything is put away, and all that Indu needs to do is her homework and study. She is angry—Indu's life should be so easy, and yet their child is unhappy. Ganesh is unhappy too—and they disagree about this very important decision. Ganesh wants to let Indu decide where she will go to school, and Hima wants them to decide as a couple. "This is too big and expensive a decision for a fourteen-year-old!" Most upsettingly, Indu has called her mother a snob, and Ganesh privately agrees with Indu.

Ganesh has hit upon a truth—Indu is not them. Many Indian families have extreme difficulty letting their children make choices and mistakes. The press of the Indian population and the extreme competitive stress of college and school admissions in India is too close for Hima to let go. She has a point when she says, "Only mad people will turn down an admission to the IITs,[15] and we should pick the best school for her, not let her make a mistake by picking the second or third best because of a whim." Ganesh wants to clarify to Hima that the pressure of Indian society is one of the reasons they live in the United States. "You hang out with too many Indian people and are getting pushed by them!" he finally says in exasperation. "I live and see it everyday at work—the 'who knows who,' the 'which school you come from,' the sheer snobbery of how much you are worth! I hate it, and I don't want it for Indu. I won't have it! Make more friends, different friends." Hima had accused him of not putting in enough thought into Indu's schooling, but she had not thought it would hit such a raw nerve, and Ganesh had not been able to clearly communicate why he held the views he did. Hima sits back for a bit. "It is difficult, you know? Every party, every weekend, the same thing. Which school are you going to, which college, who got in where, what GPA, how many APs. I feel pressure too. Poor thing, our Indu, she does not want to come to the parties these days. Poor baby." Hima rallies with the other situation she is preparing for— what if they move back to India? Should their child not be prepared to deal with that situation, too? And, they do live in their Indian community. How can they not feel the pressure? They come up with a plan to let their child speak up more about what she wants, but, even more important, prepare to hear her true voice, and help her to have courage in making a choice that may not be theirs.

I have noticed that many well-educated Indians think of their children as uncomplicated and unemotional beings. This manifests in well-meaning but inaccurately held beliefs that range from the simple to the simplistic. One is that children under the age of five don't understand and are not affected by parents' fights and angry screaming. Another is

---

[15] The IITs are premier technology education universities in India, modeled on an American curriculum but also focused completely on engineering. The IITians are viewed as top-notch engineers. Some feel that they are an elite arrogant group who take care of their own, but who may also be limited emotionally and artistically, and can't get past their own early achievements. The race and pressure to get into an IIT is immense, and children often never get over the disappointment and failure of not getting into the IITs.

expecting that teenagers who are given all the possible advantages of food, care, shelter, and the luxury of the best schools have the same values as their parents.

In this particular family, the well-intentioned parents are both overly focused on their one child's future and achievements, and do not have a space for just the couple. Indu is reacting to the immense pressure on her. She is possibly very angry that her parents have "no friends, no life" of their own and are instead looking to her to fulfill all their expectations. When parents are overly focused on their child to the exclusion of all else in their own lives, the children feel suffocated and struggle to find their own voices and expressions of personality. This was a teen exaggeration because her parents do have friends and interests apart from her, but Indu reacts angrily to her parents' needing her to be their best and not just her best.

If this situation were to be transposed to India, the teenager might not feel so much anger, for there would not be so much conflict between her values and that of the larger social world she lives in. An American educational environment is a microcosm of the larger world, where individualism is the focus more than group and family health. A child in kindergarten is not just given a piece of paper. S/he is asked what color paper s/he would like. It starts right there, where an individual's specific likes and dislikes are taken into account and assumed to be part of the personality. This same child who is asked about the smallest choices at school often has a different life at home and is given far fewer choices. The mother may be buying clothes and setting them out for the child without much or even any input from the child. The mother may be handfeeding or spoonfeeding the child meals to make sure that there is enough nutrition going in. It could be a very different world inside the home when compared to school.

Mind the gap! The London Underground's repeated warning says it all. I think there should be a good gap between children and the parents. The gap could be a small one, but one that can be bridged by the parents or the children. But the gap is essential so that there is less friction. Most Indians think the gap is too big in American homes and families. In many Indian homes, the gap is almost nonexistent. The lack of a gap often leads to stresses that build up in Indian teenagers. The parents think of "them" as "us." Another kind of gap that should be clearly understood is that between the Indian community here in the United States and the Indian community in India. When a gap does not exist between India and the Indian community here, the pressure builds up even more.

The lack of a gap is more palpable and less excusable when the family has access to more money and resources. It is easier to understand the lack when the family is struggling to make ends meet, so the pressure on the children in those situations is easy to comprehend. A family where the parents are running a restaurant or gas station has different financial pressures to deal with that more easily excuse the effort to get to the next financial and social rung of the ladder. When parents with a comfortable income and livelihood pressure their children to get up the ladder faster so it will reflect well on them, the gap is too small and causes more friction for all. It is as if the children are not good enough in themselves, and they need to be decorated with degrees from prestigious colleges that will reflect well on the parents. Children in high school are already under pressure to conform and fit in with a social structure as well as to keep up good grades. Parents are under pressure, too, and this is what is easily apparent in a casual visit to a high school open house. Adolescents need room and time to grow. They also need some structure and a good gap. A good gap would make for more comfort for all.

CHAPTER TWENTY-ONE

The Falsely Accused

The message on my voicemail was almost incoherent. After listening intently several times and trying out a few combinations of mumbled or missing digits in the phone number, I was frustrated that I could not reach the right person. I was finally able to respond to Srinath when I got an email message sent through my website. During the initial phone call, I had to ask him to slow down and repeat himself many times. It was as if he could not comprehend what I asked of him—simple basic information—and there were long pauses.

When Srinath came into my office, it took me some time to realize that he was not a teenager but was actually over forty! He was thin to the point of being emaciated, his jeans were falling off, and he nodded and shook his head whenever possible instead of speaking. Between long silences he conveyed to me that he was a software engineer working for a reputed company but that severe stress had necessitated his resigning and he now has a job in a less prestigious but still high-pressure work environment. His heavily accented English was very limited, and his tendency to swallow parts of his words made him very difficult to comprehend.

"What to do, no? Child is there and victim, and attachment is also there. So, I just am doing what judge is saying. Going to parent lessons is taking more time and work is also there. Wife is alleged that I am beating son, no? So, no use, no one believes. She is wanting to marry again and telling son she will leave if she is not having full custody. Child is victim only. I read your article[16]—you are kind and truth telling. Thank you."

As he says "thank you," he raises his clasped hands to his chest and brings it to his forehead. I get the rest of his story in between long pauses during which he looks up and away so tears don't spill out. He and his wife got married twelve years ago, had a child within a year, and he had been very happy. When misunderstandings between them grew larger than they could handle, they did not have the families nearby to help them as they would have had in India. His wife left him and returned to India, taking their two-year-old son with her without his permission. When he went back to bring them home after a few months, she would not allow him to take their son back to the United States. For the next few years, the child lived with his maternal grandparents while his mother worked in a city a night's journey away. When the child was five, she brought him back to the United States. He then took her to court and the child lived with him while she was allowed only supervised visits because the court determined that she had been neglectful and should not have kidnapped her child. After a few years of this, they both had joint custody and were officially divorced. Over the last six years, they have had a peacefully separated relationship with the child being at the center of his life. Srinath has been the soccer coach for his son's team, and has never missed a weekend with his son or shirked his responsibilities in any way. In short, according to Srinath, he has been the stable parent in his son's life. He has taken no vacations without him, and he pitches in every so often when his wife travels to visit relatives in India or "has" to go away on long spiritual retreats. He says bank records and her passport would show how much she has been away. He says further that she cries and screams whenever she wants anything from him, and that she cuts herself and has frequently threatened suicide even in front of the child. According to him, she "looks off," does not brush her hair for days, dresses poorly, and sometimes smells really bad.

---

[16] I wrote a small opinion piece for a local newspaper about the unrecognized and unintended trauma that many Indian parents inflict on their children and themselves when they leave children in India to be raised by grandparents.

According to Srinath, his wife frequently threatens their son with abandonment whenever she needs to control him in any way. Recently, his wife has alleged domestic violence by him, that he has threatened her, even though he has not been inside the same building as she has for several years, and he is now faced with the prospect of her having complete custody. She also wants to get remarried and live in India. They have been told to get counseling for parenting and domestic violence. He tells me that his wife is telling their child she will leave forever if the boy does not tell the judge that he wants to live with the mother only. Srinath understands that his son is feeling afraid of losing his mother yet again. He is paying for the child's therapy as well as following the rules by going to parenting classes. In addition, he has been asked to get counseling to address anger and parenting concerns. He denies any violence and says he could just as easily allege that she hit him. He says his wife did not allege violence until she spoke to an unethical Indian attorney. He thinks the attorney may have said it would be easier to get custody if there were a police report. He also says there are rumors about this attorney and that she is reputed to get custody at any cost. He does not step into any private space with his ex-wife and does not understand why the system favors her.

Srinath says his attorney does not do much for him, but "just he says come here, do this one, sign that one, go to classes." He does not have the savvy, money, and energy to seek and find a good family law attorney who would go to bat for him, and help him find true justice for him and his son.

The tragic situations like the above are not limited to the Indian community. But there are aspects to it that make it a more difficult situation for these immigrant families. The first difference is the absence of extended family in their immediate environment. This makes it more difficult for them to get help. When the first steps in accessing help are not available and therefore missing, it makes the next few more than a little difficult. Another difference is the reluctance to get help that is not from the family. It is almost unthinkable for many in this situation to comprehend how a mental health professional can get to know and help with the situation. In some ways, it is a simplistic understanding of the therapeutic process. It is also a complete disbelief in the possibility that an outsider can actually help the situation. There is also an absence of precedent in paying for such help. The family of the ex-wife would multiply the fee by the exchange rate (U.S. dollar to Indian Rupee) and label it too expensive. When your parents have never accessed such help, it is very hard to connect the dots and understand that a marriage in trouble wastes more money than would have been spent in paying for therapy. The nature of Western therapy, which may not be solely problem-solving, is viewed as a waste of time and money.

When a person in this situation accesses counseling help through the justice system, the person they first see is unlikely to be familiar with the Indian cultural system. If Srinath were asked by a court-appointed counselor why he allowed the child to leave the country without him, I don't think he could have explained that it was an accepted way to settle a disagreement between the couple—a wife might take a child and go back to her maternal home for a week and then there would be a way to talk with parents and others. The husband would then ask them to come back for a puja or some other social occasion as a way to bridge the differences. If he were asked if he did or did not hit his wife, he might have smiled and said, "What to do, no? I have no choice in this." This would be interpreted as "yes" by a person who does not go deeper and ask what he means by "no choice." A person like Srinath may have smiled and meant that he has no choices in life anymore, that having a child may mean he has no choices but to accept what his wife says, and that he has no options left but to say yes to anything the legal system throws at him so that he can see his son. "No choice" may also be a reference to his lifetime in the cycle of life and that things are decided for this lifetime. He has to accept his fate. He says he did tell the police that he did not hit her, but that he held her hands when she tried to hit him.

Another difference would be that in many social circles, there was no one to suggest counseling and help from the outside when the relationship was beginning to spiral out of control. Help would have come in the form of friends trying to step in to fights and counsel peace and *pujas*. Help may also come in the form of in-laws' coming to stay for a while and trying to maintain a calm atmosphere. It is unlikely that anyone would suggest professional help. Counseling along with the stigma of going to a "psychologist" becomes a last resort when things may have gone too far.

Although there are many more women who are victims of domestic violence than men, it is crucial that those who deal with families that come into the court and the legal system are aware that there are certainly many men who are falsely accused of violence and who pay a heavy price for it. I have seen many men who are married to women who look for easy and unethical ways out of situations that they do not like and cannot control. It is sometimes difficult to be a judge of who is right, but it is worth being aware of the many injustices to those falsely accused in a culture that believes women are always the "weaker sex."

The more common scenario is where the family of the man falsely accuses the woman of any of several deficiencies when they cannot control her in the usual ways.

Satish and Surya are a couple who have been married for two years. Satish is an engineer and has two older sisters who live in the United States. Surya has a younger sister who lives in India with her father. Surya's mother died of a heart attack a few months after Surya got married and moved to the United States to live with Satish. She got "sent" to me to find out why she was not "adjusting." Her husband refused to come with her saying, "I am not mad, only you are, so go and see what is wrong with you."

I meet with Surya for only a couple of sessions, and find her to be a sad young woman who is grieving over her mother's death. She says she cannot recognize herself anymore and shows me a picture of herself looking vibrant and smiling from three years ago. It turns out to be a story that is, sadly, only too common. She was not "allowed" to go home when her mother died because his family said it was more important for his parents to visit their son at the same time, and she needed to be there to help them and cook for them. They did not like that "she had a sad face all the time" and wanted her to study for her exams so she could get a job as a doctor soon and start earning some of her keep. When her in-laws visit, she sees with shock that her mother-in-law gets Satish to give her daily massages for her aching back. Her sisters-in-law call every day asking what she cooked for dinner, tell her where to buy rotis [flat unleavened bread], ask her what soap she uses for laundry, and tell her how to starch Satish's shirts. When they see her crying after talking to her sister, they tell her to call less often. Satish gives her only enough money each day for essentials, and gets upset when she asks for money to get her eyebrows shaped, telling her that women in his family don't go to beauty parlors. This is clearly a cruel family that views her as domestic help until she can start earning money.

Surya does not tell her father what is going on because he is already having a difficult time after losing his wife. She does not tell her sister much either because her sister is studying for exams, but she has guessed that Surya is really unhappy. Surya is also acutely aware that if she leaves the marriage, it will impact her sister's chances of finding a good arranged match because relatives would want to know why the older sister is divorced and conservative families would want an unsullied family. When Satish finds a reason to slap her, Surya calls a domestic violence agency and talks to an Indian woman there. To her utter shock, she goes home and finds the agency worker talking to her husband, and together they threw her things out into the street. Luckily for Surya, she had her passport with her, as she needed it as proof of identity to file papers for her exam application.

Satish had fabricated a whole story of how Surya was mad and had threatened him. He tells her he will tell everyone in India that she is unstable and has been in "psychiatric" care. Surya was so terrified during our second meeting that she started at every sound in the office. She had spent the night at a hotel using her Indian credit card and left her passport with me for safekeeping. The only redeeming factor in what is a shockingly common story was that her father was supportive and asked her to come home immediately when she called him from my office. It also helped that her sister was in love with a fellow student and was unlikely to enter the traditional arranged marriage route. Surya offers to mail me my fee from India, but I don't have the heart to accept a fee and instead ask her to donate something to a women's shelter in India. A friend she met through the exam prep classes offers to help her buy a ticket and get her to the airport.

This happened to a smart well-educated woman who had family support. It is horrifying to imagine the plight of women who have fewer means, education, family options, and abilities, and have to further contend with restrictive visa limitations. This kind of occurrence is not rare, and almost all my Indian friends have heard of or know someone who has been through such ordeals. Certainly, more women are abused than men, and I estimate the ratio of falsely accused men to women to be in the range of 1:15. It is even sadder that the women who access help tend to be educated and with earning potential. The women who are dependent on visas that are connected to their husbands' don't have the ability to get a job and make their own money, and so are much less likely to get help. That number drops even further if there is a child in their lives.

An equally sad but different situation arises when a person who needs mental-health care refuses to get it and hides the fact from a new spouse. Aruna had met Karthik two or three times in India, and the match had been suggested by mutual friends. Aruna thought Karthik was somewhat quiet and introverted, but he seemed helpful and interested in her wanting a career of her own. Karthik seemed very interested in what she liked and she expected that they would talk more once they were engaged. During the engagement period when she was still in India waiting for her papers to be processed, she realized Karthik was unwilling to talk much on the phone and was very busy. She ascribed it to a busy lifestyle and his general quiet nature.

Once she came to live with him, she realized things were very different than she had imagined. He was quite paranoid and imagined people were trying to listen to their conversations. He was very rigid in his ways and had to shop only in certain aisles of stores. He refused to meet friends of hers and was suspicious of her interest in movie stars and rock musicians. She soon grew isolated and afraid especially when he insisted she only talk on the phone in his presence and on his cell phone. Aruna's dreams of studying flew out the window, and soon her sole preoccupation was devising ways to figure a way out of her prison. His parents insisted that nothing was wrong and that things would be okay once they had children. Marriage and a family should fix his loneliness, which, according to them, was the cause of his being stressed. She was astounded that they knew of his condition and were unwilling to confront it or even consider other treatments. She fled the home and country with the help of friends and considered herself lucky. She later heard he had remarried into yet another marriage arranged to make him better. What added insult to injury was his family's insistence that if she had been a patient and loving wife, things would have been okay eventually, and it then became that she was falsely accused of being too selfish and impatient in wanting a "normal" relationship.

All the above scenarios are tragic in that the old prescriptions and ways of finding out about a potential family match fall apart because of geographical distance and a different, more anonymous, way of life in the United States. The same things could have happened in India, and possibly still do, but there are usually people around who know something of what goes on and the families are not too far away and able to help if they have the economic means, education, and the will to confront wrongs.

CHAPTER TWENTY-TWO

For Here? or To Go?

For immigrating Indians, living in the new country is a balancing
act. When a family moves to the United States from India, they
bring with them hopes and dreams, as well as fears and guilt.
Their hopes and dreams, combined with hard work, pay off with a better
lifestyle than they would have had in the home country, on top of increased wealth and status. The fears and guilt serve as a counterbalance.

Raja and Renu are a couple from South India with one child. They
are an immigrant success story. Over the last twenty years they have
emerged from middle class backgrounds to become some of the wealth-
iest people in Silicon Valley. Although their money gives them a lot of
freedom, they struggle with the same issues that a lot of other Indian
families deal with. Raja feels very conflicted about living in the United
States. Renu misses life in India. But they feel compelled to give their
child the best of both worlds. So they shuttle back and forth spending
time between the two worlds. While there is nothing wrong with this,
they don't seem at peace with all they have.

Raja shakes his head from side to side and insists, "I will not die in
this country. I want water from the Ganga in the minutes before my
death." Renu chides him for being morbid—"Why think about death
now? There is so much more to worry about, daughter and education
and marriage... all this dying talk is for later, no?" She moves on to
more mundane worries. She worries that their daughter will not get into

the best schools because "she is having too much fun and not studying enough." They both feel a lot of guilt about not being around their family in India as much as they should. Raja and Renu treat their friends and families cordially and do not fail to keep the courtesies they grew up with. They personally cook food for their friends, invite them over, and talk after dinner about how kids these days don't understand the value of hard work.

Recently, Raja has begun to talk about waiting for their child to go to college and then retiring to India. They want a good life for her, but feel immense sadness that their child will not have all their values—she might not understand that she should think about her parents and in-laws when she marries—will her husband treat them (his in-laws) well? They have realized their hopes and dreams in material ways, but live with guilt and fear in their everyday lives.

Renu does not want to move back to India permanently. She treasures her freedom here in the United States, where prying eyes and listening ears do not broadcast her every move. She has learned to enjoy the anonymity that life here provides—she knows, for example, that her in-laws' maid is not going to tell them that she had friends over on a day when she could have visited them.

Raja has ideas about death and end of life issues that he feels are in conflict with the larger culture here. He believes that people in India will take better care of elders compared with people here. He believes he should be with his parents as they age and become feeble. But he also feels the pull of exciting technology, a system that works so products can be made quickly and ideas executed, and an easier day-to-day life. They want their daughter, in particular, to be raised with and around Indian values. His wife and daughter are happier here, and they have a circle of Indian friends to spend weekends with. Renu also feels some of this guilt of not caring enough for her parents, but she has a brother who lives in India and she lets him carry the lion's share of caring for her parents.

Most Indians are not in similar positions where they can rent a jet to fly back at a moment's notice, but most will relate to Raja and Renu and at least identify with their quandary as they try to arrive at a place of balance and acceptance. Raja and Renu have committed to a life of shuttling between two worlds quite fluidly. They send their child to an international school in India, so she can live close to both sets of grandparents and spend the summers in the United States enjoying summer camps and practicing Indian music. Raja and Renu take turns visiting their daughter and parents every month, believing they have the best of both worlds. Their daughter however, is not cooperating any more, and she wants to live in one place and hang out with a stable set of friends. She wants to be "normal" like her American friends and is angry that her parents can't see what she wants. She accuses them of living in India's past and in their own yesterdays. "India has changed, the kids do worse things there than they do here, but my parents have their heads in the sand," she complains bitterly. The daughter is petulant; "Why can't they just let me be me," she complains in a very American individual-first manner.

The "n +2" is at the other end of the spectrum from the family above. A young person or family who moves to the United States are said to be in the "n+2 phase" when they are considering going back to India in a couple of years. The "n" refers to the point in time they are at and it is a moving target that changes with every year. This postponement of a huge life decision unfortunately keeps them from committing to a life either here or in India. This is evident in small things such as keeping the children learning at the level they would be learning if they were in India.

Preeti is busy every weekend shuttling her children to and from a religious school so they can keep up with Indian values, as well as language class so that the children can keep up with the same textbooks that are used at their level in India. She gets the textbooks from Indian schools every year and has the children work with a tutor so that they can keep up with their Indian peers. Thus, when and if they move back, the children will not have to struggle with lost language skills. Preeti feels considerable anxiety about not having made a decision. She is the only child of her parents and would like to live close to them. Her husband is the younger son of medical doctors and his older brother shares in their practice, so he does not feel a need to move back any time soon. Mathematics—seen as a gateway subject that leads to higher-paying jobs—is an especially fraught topic because there is a different emphasis on quick recall and memorization in India. Indians, in general, have considerable anxiety when their children do not do well in math. Math and language skills become part of the balancing act when a family does not or cannot make a commitment to live in one country or the other. When combined with the n+2 sitting-on-the-fence, this leads to additional stress for the family.

Buying a house is a more accepted way of making a commitment to stay in the United States. It is common for disagreements to arise within the couple after they make the decision to buy. If one or the other of the couple feels they have compromised on their values in actually buying a home, that person tends to be more sensitive to feelings of being taken advantage of in other interactions between the couple. A move into the new home can bring up acute feelings of having abandoned the parent generation in India. If the parents in India do not clearly state that they want their children to come back and live in India, the immigrant generation takes it on themselves to feel the ambivalence and the accompanying stress. When the parents are clear and say to their children something like, "You should live there (USA) where life is easier and you are happy with your jobs," the immigrant adult children feel a sense of doing the right thing for themselves, and help the parents with money and the comforts it can buy.

Some families do their duty towards their parents and also assuage their own feelings of guilt and shame by buying a home or flat in India that their parents can live in (rent-free, of course). This allows for several things at once. It may or not be a good financial investment, but it is a foothold in India if things go wrong in their life in the United States. It becomes a psychological home that is there and waiting as a sort of insurance policy. Some people think that the cost of healthcare may be unaffordable in the United States by the time they retire and then having a home base in India helps with "medical tourism." Having a home in India, as long as the family has the means to have a relative live in or near it to monitor its upkeep, may be a practical plan. If the parents are living in the home, it becomes a way for everyone to benefit—the parents feel helpful and useful and the adult children feel they are making a contribution in the right direction.

In the absence of a concrete and planned move back to India, some families drift in and out of a plan until the children get to an age where a move back is more difficult. Then, the decision is made by not making one. Manoj and Manju have two children and have many arguments and disagreements about a plan to move back to India. Manju has high blood pressure and migraines that are disabling. Manoj has had difficulty in his work life as a marketing manager because he has to help Manju so many times a week with picking up children and dinner that his work day in interrupted. He has had to give up his art and music classes and feels his life is out of balance. Manju talks about how angry she is with him because she was ready to move "back home" five years ago, and now she is worried for her daughter who has friends here and is looking forward to high school. She is also concerned that her daughter will be really unhappy with the Indian way of teaching. For herself, Manju worries that in India she will be completely occupied with managing servants and drivers, and will not have personal time. Her daily life is very peaceful here and she does not have to deal with in-laws and relatives visiting at all hours and needing to be fed and entertained. According to her, Manoj was trying to time the markets just right and they missed the opportune window. When Manoj was able to convince Manju that she could have a "job" to go to and that he would manage relatives, she was ready to consider what it would take to make the move. She was able to talk to the children about the positives about a move to India, and was more able to face the prospect when the family decided that after high school in India, they would consider sending their daughter to college in the United States. According to her, everything would have been easier if they had moved when the children were less than ten years old. She is also sure that if the move does not work out, it will be final for both of them—they will not have hope anymore about the possibility of moving back—and a final reality that they would always live in the United States. That somehow seemed to be a very difficult thing to consider. It was better to keep the hope alive than to face commitment and certainty.

The heart of the matter for many of these families seems to be the idea of India as a fallback plan, an insurance safety net after making a nest-egg amount of money in the United States—an ideal that may not actually exist. In addition, many of the families who live in limbo have a romanticized idea of the India they left and not a genuine, cold-light-of-day view of the India that is in the here and now. Home is never the same after having left it once, and the decision to stay or go becomes a complicated grieving and a multi-faceted situation that can't be simply solved.

CHAPTER TWENTY-THREE

A Certain Smile

A t first I titled this last chapter of the book, "Help Wanted." My plan was to describe the different ways Indians in the United States access help from the psychotherapeutic community. But, as I wrote it, it seemed not to fit in with the tone of the rest of the book. So, instead, I decided to write a personal goodbye note to you, the reader. So, "A Certain Smile" turns out to be a more suitable title.

Many years ago, as I sat with a group of distinguished doctors, psychiatrists, neurologists, and clinicians in Palo Alto, California, I was astonished by a scene that unfolded in front of me. As a colleague presented a case about a young married Indian couple and some of their difficulties, one of the clinicians smiled when the presenter said that the couple had had an arranged marriage after their horoscopes were matched up by the family's personal astrologer. The smile stayed with me for a very long time. It was a smile of amusement, disbelief, and condescension.

Horoscopes have a very different meaning and significance in India than they do in the West. They are astrological charts that use complex mathematical formulae to calculate, (based on the time of birth, latitude, and longitude of the person's place of birth), the positions of the sun, the moon, and planets at the precise moment of birth. These charts have information about the person's life. The positions of the sun, moon, and several planets are all believed to have an influence on the person's life. It is widely believed that accurate predictions can be made about people—their personality, their interests, their interactions, their achievements, and their family—depending on the ability (combining art and science) of the person who casts and reads the charts. When there is a belief in the larger Indian community that everything has been pre-ordained and metaphorically prewritten "on the forehead," this attempt to decipher and make the best of your life is well-founded. Many families believe that matching horoscopes is an essential addition to considering the similarities of family background and expectations in making a matrimonial match.

But I wondered if the "smiler" had understood "horoscope" as extrapolated from, and connected to, the entertaining "prediction for the day" in the daily newspaper. It matters not at all if the clinician believed in it or not. It was hugely important that the couple sitting in front of a therapist be understood and not smiled at (even internally) for their beliefs and way of life. The smile spoke volumes to me. And so I began to write this book, for I saw that help was needed in a very different way in the therapeutic community that deals with the Indian population, but knows little about it.

Similarly, at another case presentation, a family from another culture was being discussed, and some of the diagnosis was that there was an obsessive-compulsive component in the washing of cardboard and plastic milk cartons after they were purchased and before they were put away in the refrigerator. What I know from living in India and being somewhat aware of the rituals of daily life is that milk sachets arrive at the market place and are sometimes splashed with mud and dirt from being transported (sometimes on bicycles) and most people would wash the packages before they would open or store them. While it is possible that the patient did indeed have an obsessive-compulsive disorder, this piece of information alone was not enough to make a diagnosis. It may have been that the person was acting in a culturally appropriate manner in taking care of her family.

When a visiting family member was taken ill and complained of chest pain, we rushed her to the doctor. Of course, all six of us went with her. The doctor on call did not appreciate that the whole family arrived with the patient and made a negative comment about it. She did not understand that this was a way of showing support and love for the patient. There is a general understanding in India that the patient and the person closest to the patient are under a lot of stress during a hospital visit and may not remember all of the doctor's instructions or even be able to clearly communicate the events that led to the visit. In addition to moral and family support, the family members also serve a very practical purpose—one person may go get the medication prescribed, another take care of the food, and another may take the patient straight back home to rest immediately. Extra bodies are good for the patient, and would have also allowed for better medical care. The culture holds that it is a terrible misfortune to be all alone, and the family coming to the doctor is understood to provide moral support to the patient.

An understanding chuckle, with, "Lots of people care for you, Mrs. X! Let's see if we can have just one or two others in the room, and I can come back and speak to all of you ..." would have gone a long way to help the family feel less alienated. If the doctor felt under additional pressure from scrutiny by the family, it is understandable that she could not support the family while being defensive.

The book is built on stories I wanted to tell with the "smiler" in mind. These stories are meant to encourage you to listen to the person in front of you instead of the pathology, to suggest that you stay with curiosity instead of going to a reflexive response to cleanse the symptoms, and to invite you into the inner world of your Indian clients—a world inseparable from and shaped by their families and their cultural beliefs, habits, principles, and values. I hope the stories I have told stay with you in some form or another, and have helped you understand the Indian community a little better than you did before you went through these pages.

Glossary

Ahimsa—Non-violence. See Vegetarianism.

Ammah —Mother. Also used to swear in disbelief if spoken emphatically.

Appah —Father. Also used to swear in disbelief if spoken emphatically.

Arjuna—Important in the telling of the *Bhagavad Gita*. One of the five Pandava Princes, Arjuna was the greatest warrior and was crucial to the Pandava victory over the Kauravas. His skill with the bow and arrow was unmatched. He engages with Lord Krishna during the war to understand the primary importance of carrying out his duties.

Arre!—Exclamation in Hindi, which means anything from a hello to an angry response.

Artha—Means of life, livelihood, money, and physical security. It is one of the four important aims of human life according to Hinduism and encompasses meaning, sense, goal and purpose. It can allow for people to strive for a living and make money, collect art, or engage in other forms of an attached life. It is also connected to *Dharma, Kama,* and *Moksha,* and combined with all of them, becomes a way to bridge the different aspects of life. A person should do the right thing according to their family obligations (*dharma,*) try to make a living and provide for self and family in terms of money and security (*artha*), be emotionally, sensually and physically fulfilled (*kama*), and then look towards a good life aiming towards self-realization (*moksha*.) The words can actually be linked together in Sanskrit as *dharmarthakamamoksha*, and the linking of the words suggests they are part of a person's right life. I understand *Artha* as a duty-bound striving towards thriving in life, and a rite of life passage.

Ayyo —A Tamil expression of loss, shock, or distress, variously used to show worry or surprise depending on the tone of expression.

Bhagavad Gita*—The Mahabharata*, or the great story of *Bharat* (India or land of *Bharata*), is one of the two major epics of India. It is the story, with many stories nested inside, of the families of a king. Warring cousins, powerful mothers, helpful gods, and moral struggles all go into making this a most fascinating story where all manner of Hindu ideals and struggles play out. The heart of the story is the righteous war fought between the five *Pandava* princes and their 100 *Kaurava* cousins. The eldest of the *Pandava* princes who does not know he is a *Pandava* (his then unmarried virgin mother secretly gave him up at birth) fights for the *Kauravas* who accept him. The five princes who humbly ask the god *Krishna* (by sitting at his feet while the *Kauravas* sit at his head while he slept) for help in the war. The *Kauravas* get *Krishna's* army while the *Pandavas* humbly ask that *Krishna* be their charioteer.

The god *Krishna* acts as charioteer to the *Pandavas*, and his sermon to the *Pandava* Prince *Arjuna* during a battle forms the *Bhagavad Gita*, which translates to "Song of God." *Arjuna*, the bravest and best warrior prince, loses heart and declares that he cannot go into battle and kill cousins who were his childhood playmates or his old teachers. *Arjuna* hears from *Krishna* about his royal duties, his *dharma*, and his goal to focus on the right actions without attachment to the outcomes (of the war).

The *Bhagavad Gita* forms the backbone of philosophic Hindu ideals. The best *dharmic* principles proscribe doing one's duty without attachment to the results. Letting go of the outcome but still doing one's duty is understood to be an ideal for every person, even godly princes. Duty and ethics, right and wrong, purpose and destiny, and intentions of good for the larger world, versus personal struggle and moral ambivalence, are all discussed in this discourse.

It is said to date from the 4th to 2nd Century BCE, but is a remembered story and not a written one, and as such evolved over time. Most Hindu homes have a depiction of this *Gita* in artistic form—usually showing the blue-skinned god Krishna holding the reins of the chariot in one hand while he turns and addresses the Prince *Arjuna,* who has his powerful weapon of bow and arrow in hand, but who is filled with doubt about the right way. The understanding that comes from the *Gita* is that the god *Krishna* himself said one must do one's duty even it is something that is morally difficult, if it is for the greater good.

Bhakti—*Bhakti* is a spiritual love and participatory devotion towards religious concepts or principles. It is one of the many *yogas* or paths towards *moksha*. Other paths are through doing works of charity and service, through knowledge, or through meditation. *Bhakti* is an intense devotion that is transcendental and that lifts one up out of the ordinary. *Bhakti* can be felt towards a teacher, a god, a spiritual ideal, or meditation, and is understood to produce bliss.

The experience of *Bhakti* is to be so immersed in the feeling that it takes one out of, and beyond oneself. It is an immersive experience whether the relationship is a parent-child, a friend to friend, human to god, or without form.

Bhai—Brother in Hindi. An older brother or a more respectful term would be *Bhaiyya*. Addressing a man as *bhai* even in everyday interactions with strangers is considered courteous. A young woman may address the taxi driver as *bhai* if he is young or as an uncle or grandfather (many words are available in different languages.) Similarly a woman may be addressed as *behen* (sister) or as an aunt or grandmother in courteous speech.

Bharat—India or land of *Bharata*.

Bharat Ratna—India's most meritorious civilian award (India's Jewel) and honor from the Republic of India for exceptional service, endeavor, or performance of the highest order. It is awarded without bias as to race, occupation, or gender.

Bindi—See *Kumkum*

Brahma—*Brahma* is the creator god and is the third of the trinity of *Brahma*, *Vishnu* and *Shiva*. *Brahma* creates, *Vishnu* preserves and *Shiva* destroys—so that the world is in balance. Brahma is depicted with four faces. He is rarely worshipped in India and only two temples to him exist. He is depicted sitting on a lotus. His consort *Saraswati* is the goddess of learning, music, and wisdom. There is also an idea that he is not worshiped as he married his creation.

Brahmins—Highest strata in the caste system made up of priests and scholars.

Deepavali or **Diwali**—*Deepavali* is a festival of light, celebrated on the darkest night of the new moon between October and November. The actual date varies on the Gregorian calendar but is decided according to the Hindu calendar, which follows lunar and solar cycles. The customs can vary according to the communities and states, but the unifying aspects are the same. It is the victory of good over evil, light over darkness, hope over dread, and renewal of ties in families. Lamps are lit all over the homes and streets, firecrackers set off, sweets are made and shared, new clothes are worn, homes are cleaned, friends and families are invited to share time, food, and traditions, and a new period begins.

In some communities, the most important goddess of wealth—*Lakshmi*—is worshiped and welcomed to the home. Some others celebrate the return of Prince *Rama* (an incarnation of *Vishnu*), his wife *Seetha* and brother *Lakshmana* from the forest, after 14 years of exile and after the defeat of the ten-headed demon king *Ravana*. Other communities celebrate the goddess *Kali* or *Durga* and her killing of a powerful demon. In *Tamilnadu*, *Deepavali* is celebrated because god *Krishna* kills the demon *Naraka*.

In most communities, there is a special family celebration—spanning a few days to a week—for newlywed couples, a renewal of sibling and brother-sister bonds, and occasion to celebrate and renew life. It can be understood as Christmas and New Year combined.

Desi—From the home country. This informally includes Pakistan, Sri Lanka, and Bangladesh.

Deyvittu—In god's name.

Dharma—*Dharma* means a life of duty. Doing one's duty is the highest goal of a devout Hindu. A dutiful husband, wife, son, daughter, or parent takes great pride in doing his or her utmost to live up to the ideals imposed on them by society. *Dharma* encompasses the right way of living—holding ideals, duties, laws, customs, religious duties, behaviors, with the larger order of society and family in mind.

Dharma is difficult to translate. One cannot think of *Dharma* for oneself individually. *Dharma* only exists in connection to others in the family and community. I think of *Dharma* as a way of holding firm to ideals, wishes, and goals for the larger good, as possible, and embodied through me.

Drishti or Nazar—The evil eye's energy. An envious glance or envy felt or imagined can also set in motion what a family may do to ward off the negative energy. Some families take lemons and green chilies and add salt to it, waving it around the person's head and then throw it away along with the collected bad luck. Complimenting a child is sometimes thought to lead to bad luck or the evil eye. Some people wear amulets blessed by a god around the upper arm. Sometimes babies have *kajal* or cooling eyeliner applied to their eyes or as a spot on the cheek to ward off negative energy coming their way.

Ganesha—*Ganesha* is the popular, much loved and adored god of new beginnings. He is pot-bellied, rides on a mouse, has an elephant head, and four arms. In one of his depictions, he carries a piece of his broken tusk with which shows he is the divine scribe. In another, he tastes a delicious dumpling. He also carries a lotus and a string of beads. Other depictions portray him dancing or playing an instrument. As a fairly new god, who grew popular in 3rd or 4th Century A.D., he has proved accessible and changeable in form to his devotees. He is the granter of wishes and is prayed to at the start of all new beginnings.

Ganesha was created by his mother *Parvati* out of clay or rubbings from her own body. He was on duty to guard her and denied his father *Shiva* access to her. *Shiva* was enraged and cut off his head. When *Parvati* found out, she was furious. *Shiva* was sorry and he sent out to have the head found. The only head found was that of an elephant, and so Shiva set that on the child's head and *Ganesha* was thus revived.

Ganges—India's sacred river that rises in the Western Himalayas and flows through North India and Bangladesh, emptying into the Bay of Bengal. The river and goddess *Ganga* are worshiped by Hindus, and thus the river has cultural and religious significance. After cremation, ashes are brought to be immersed in the waters of the *Ganga* to improve chances of eternal salvation. The power of the *Ganga* was so fierce that she had to be tamed by landing first in *Shiva's* matted locks of hair. Dying on the banks of the *Ganga* is thought to lead to immediate *moksha*.

Gori—*Gora* in Hindi means white or pale and *gori* is the feminine use of the word. In casual usage in the united States, it refers to any Caucasian or white-appearing person and does not distinguish if the person is of any particular class within white society. It is more of a cultural term in that sense, without defining if the person is from New York or Alabama. In using the term *Gora* or *Gori*, it is understood that the person is a cultural 'other,' not being a *desi*.

Jadoo—Magic by literal translation but referring to witchcraft or the evil eye. See also **Drishti**.

Jataka—A *Jataka* is a horoscope. In many communities of India, when a child is born, a horoscope is cast for him or her. The piece of paper on which it is written is called the "*Vedic* horoscope of *jataka*." It considers the position of the moon, the sun, and different planets at the exact time, date, and longitude of birth. It is then put away to be read by a skilled astrologer who can predict many aspects of the child's life. A good astrologer will predict the personality of the child, closeness to a relative, success in school, life, and relationships. Often, marriage arrangements are made after the horoscopes of the "boy" and "girl" are matched by a skilled astrologer. The astrologer is a wise person who is considered a learned person, one who casts light that is not visible to others. The astrologer takes into account bad periods in one's life as foretold by the horoscope, and balances it with the horoscope of one whose life it evens out. If too many points do not match, or one's horoscope impacts the other's life negatively, the astrologer will reject the match. Numerous accounts are related in every family of events that prove the accuracy of the forecast by the astrologer. As always, there are unlucky and bad events that occur; and then the astrologer usually explains that forces beyond comprehension may have marred his or her vision.

The question is not one of truth and accuracy of prediction but of faith, belief, and the community values that go into the religious, social, and cultural contexts of looking into the future as much as possible in order to make the best of life and reduce worry. Some communities and families believe in astrology more than others and, accordingly, weigh their decisions by social, familial, economic, and other factors when they make big life choices.

Kama—*Kama* refers to emotional, sensual, and pleasurable fulfillment. *Kama Deva* is the god of love who shoots arrows of flowers, which trigger desire. *Kama* refers to love, sex, desire, longing, sensual pleasure, aesthetic enjoyment of art, dance, music, and other arts, and is considered one of the worthy goals of life along with *Artha*, *Dharma* and *Moksha*. *Kama* can be understood as the finding of an object, the finding of pleasure in it, and of melding with it in harmony of body and soul so that one is fulfilled. It is a love that is in accord with *Dharma*, *Artha*, and *Moksha*, and is uplifting, right, and necessary to wellbeing. The *Kama Sutra*, which is the ancient Hindu manual of love, is only partly about sexual pleasures, but mostly about the philosophy and theory of love.
See also **Artha**.

Kali—See **Deepavali or Diwali**

Karma—*Karma* is an outcome of *Dharma*. Doing your *dharmic* duties gets you good merits or good *karma* in your present life and in your future lives. Your challenges and blessings in your current life can be understood as not just luck, but as direct *karma* from your doings and *dharma* in your past lives.

Believing in *karma* is a clear association with believing in rebirth of the soul in different bodies over many lifetimes. The blooming lotus is a symbol of *karma* in the Hindu tradition.

Kaurava—Gandhari, who lived voluntarily blindfolded with her sight-less husband Dhritharashtra (a descendent of the Kurus) was granted a boon by sage Vyasa. She asked for 100 sons and one daughter, who were all grown and born from one lump of flesh. These one hundred brothers were the *Kauravas.* Dhritharashtra also had one more son through a *Vaishya* or trader-caste woman. The brothers were the proverbial wicked children and the counterpoint to the *Pandava* princes, who were all that was noble in the world. Duryodhana, the oldest of the *Kaurava* princes, was a powerful villain in *The Mahabharata.* He befriends Karna (the older brother of the *Pandavas* who was fathered by the sun god Surya, but abandoned at birth by his mother as she was unmarried at the time) and befriends him. Then Karna fights against his biological half-brothers by joining the *Kauravas.* The *Kaurava* brothers cheat, steal, and try to ignobly kill their cousins the *Pandavas* many times. They also insult the *Pandava* queen Draupadi (married to the five *Pandava* princ-es) in their court, incurring the wrath of *Arjuna,* who swears to kill the one hundred brothers. These stories are part of *The Mahabharata.*

Krishna—One of the incarnations of *Vishnu. Krishna's* mother was imprisoned by her brother and all her children were systematically killed. *Krishna* was born late at night, to his virgin mother through *Vishnu's* agency; and the gates of the jail magically opened, the rivers parted their waters, and the infant was swapped and raised among the cowherds. The mother who raised him was Yashoda and *Krishna* is often depicted as a young child, stealing and eating butter, and then opening his mouth to show Yashoda the whole universe in it. In his incarnation as *Krishna,* he performs miraculous feats like killing a serpent that terrorized the town by dancing on its head, by killing the evil woman who tried to suckle him, and by sheltering the whole town from a storm by holding up a mountain above them. (In *Vishnu's* incar-nation as *Rama,* he was more of a royal, mortal king.) *Krishna* is also worshiped and depicted as a god who satisfies all the women who adore him; the playful protector of the cowherds, as the timeless, immortal, devoted partner of Radha (RadhaKrishna are together considered a godhead as their union was divine and selfless, but unmarried); and

then in his form of the god providing sage counsel to *Arjuna* in the *Bhagavad Gita* part of *The Mahabharata*. *Krishna* means dark, and in his youthful form, he is depicted as a dark-skinned or blue-skinned god with cows around him, playing a flute to entrance the gopis who took care of the cows, and with peacock feathers in his hair.
See also Mahabharata, Ramayana, Vishnu.

Kshatriyas—In the caste system, *Kshatriyas* is the second stratum below the Brahmins. These are the warriors. The royalty were most often *Kshatriyas*, and were allowed to eat meat, and to marry Brahmins.

Kumkum or Bindi—The red (or other colour) dot worn on the middle of the forehead and between the brows is called a *Bindi*. It used to be made up *kumkum*, a red powder that was made with powdered turmeric and lime. The location of the sixth chakra or third eye is believed to be between the eyebrows, and putting this powder at that location was a way to draw attention to a holy spot. Pressing turmeric (believed to have healing and antiseptic properties) on that spot was also a way to draw one's own as well as others' attention to one's inner power.

It is now most commonly worn by Hindu women at all times, but men also wear *kumkum* after *puja* or on festive occasions. Some communities wear a white U symbol to depict *Vishnu* devotion with a red mark in the middle. Another community of Iyers wear three horizontal stripes across the forehead (of white ash), with a red dot in the middle, to show their faith in *Shiva* the destroyer.

In North India, young women wear *kumkum* after they get married, and also wear it in their hair parting. In South India, all young women wear *kumkum*. Most Hindus wear it as a symbol of faith, piety, fashion, and to show they have families who care for them. It used to be that widows could not wear *kumkum* and were not offered *kumkum*. The offering of *kumkum* to every female member of a party after a visit is an informal blessing and expression of hope for continued goodwill and good fortune.

Lakshmana— See **Deepavali or Diwali**; *also see* **the Ramayana**.

Lakshmi—See **Vishnu** and **Lakshmi**.

Lasya— Graceful and beautiful dance of the goddess *Parvati* in response to the powerful cosmic dance of the cycle of life and death (Tandava) performed by god *Shiva*.

Mahabharata, The—One of the two major epics from Hindu India. It is the story of a family divided by warring cousins. It contains the *Bhagavad Gita*, which speaks of the different aspects of *yogas*—of devotion, duty, action, piety—that make for a good life. It is full of parables, morals, and depictions of different aspects of life, comprising a source of thousands of stories. The *Pandava* princes fight against their evil *Kaurava* cousins and win a war that paves the way for a righteous life. The human *Pandava* princes are guided by the god *Krishna,* who is an avatar or incarnation of *Vishnu*, the god of preservation. *Krishna* performs miracles in his childhood, kills demons, and shows himself in his true form—brighter than a thousand suns—to *Arjuna* the *Pandava* prince during his discourse of the *Bhagavad Gita*.
See also **Bhagavad Gita**

Moksha **or** *Nirvana*—The ultimate goal of a soul is to be released from the cycles of birth, death and rebirth. When the soul is set free forever, it attains *Moksha* (more used in Hinduism) or *nirvana* (typically more used in Buddhism). A highly enlightened and self-realized being is understood to be able to die at will and move on from this cycle of birth, death, and rebirth. The cycle is called *Samsara*, and *Moksha* is the release from a life of sins, suffering, rebirths and testing. A complete faith in god (pure devotion or *Bhakti*) also moves one along in the path to *Moksha*.

Moksha is also the fourth and last goal of every human life as understood in Hinduism. The first three are *Dharma, Artha,* and *Kama*. The concept of *Moksha* has evolved over time with the interpretations of many Hindu philosophers, but it remains an ideal state of most devout Hindus.

Murugan—Hindu god of war. Murugan is the younger son of Shiva and Parvati, younger brother of Ganesha. His vehicle is the peacock and he carries a spear. He was born of the spark from Shiva's third eye, and carried by six lotuses, and then the stars (the Pleiades) as even the fire god Agni could not contain him. Parvati then unites them into one child, whom she brings to Shiva as their son. Murugan is popular in south India and in Sri Lanka, Singapore, and Malaysia among the Tamil-speaking populations.

Namaskaram—See **Pranam or Namaste**

Namaste—*Namaste* is a greeting or leave-taking gesture. Palms are pressed together, thumbs closest to the body, and raised to a bowed head, forehead, or chest. It is the same gesture that is used for worship in temples and to gods, goddesses, and people. It is a gesture of humility and for a greeting, goodbye, or expression of gratitude. *Namaste* translates to "I bow to the divine in you."

Naraka and *Svarga*—Naraka is considered a space in limbo where one's soul languishes for a time as a result of bad actions in the lifetime just past. Depending on the severity of the act, one could stay in this dark hellish place before being shunted to another lifetime, where one would continue to pay for or merit from one's previous actions. *Svarga* is the heavenly counterpart of *Naraka,* where one reaps rewards of good behavior in past lives before being reborn or attaining *Moksha.* They are sometimes understood to be metaphorical, although always temporary.

Nirvana—See **Moksha**

Paavam and *Punyam*—These are terms of extreme wickedness or goodness. In North India they are also known as *Paap* and *Punya.* An extreme bad act changes the balance of your *Karmic* inheritance. *Paavam* is doing something evil and wicked, such as killing something without reason or going against family values by hurting someone, which would tilt the balance; and the expectation is that you would pay for it in some way in your future or in a future lifetime. On the other hand, *punyam* refers to acts of extreme goodness that would get you positive merits in this life or in the next lifetime.

Pandava—The Pandavas are the five noble brothers who are sons of King Pandu. The first three are Yudhishtira the noble, Bhima the strong, and Arjuna the brave. They are born to King Pandu's wife Kunti through Yama, the god of death, Vayu, the god of wind and air, and Indra, the god of sky and war respectively. Kunti also had a son Karna, whom she abandoned at birth after he was fathered by the sun god, Surya. Karna later fights against his (half) brothers, the Pandavas, by joining the Kaurava forces. The other two Pandava princes are born to Pandu's second wife Madri, and fathered by the celestial Ashwini twins. Together, the five princes marry one princess—Draupadi, obeying their mother's command to share what Arjuna had won in a bridal contest. Arjuna beheads Karna during the war, and when they find out who Karna was, the Pandavas almost lose their will to rule their kingdom after victory.

Parvati—*Parvati* (or *Shakti*) is *Shiva's* female counterpart. She is the mother goddess and symbolizes fertility, grace, strength, love, abundance, and devotion. She is re-born many times and her consort is always *Shiva*. She has at least a thousand names and reciting her names is a prayer in its own right. In her fearsome aspects she is *Durga* or *Kali*, riding a tiger with ten arms with weapons, fiercely protecting, although with one hand raised in a benevolent gesture.

Parvati is often worshipped with *Shiva* and depicted as the *yoni* or womb from which a phallic symbol emerges. They are also depicted as an androgynous form of half-man and half-woman. Erotic sculptures often represent *Shiva* and *Parvati* and also the marriage of cosmic forces such as light and darkness, earth and sky, and spirit and substance. See also **Shiva**.

Pranam **or** *Namaskaram*—*Pranam* or *Namaskaram* is a gesture sometimes accompanying the gesture of *Namaste*, where the person offering the *Namaste* also lies flat on the floor, with the forehead touching the ground, or in a half-prostration with the knees, forehead, and hands on the floor. It is a more formal and whole- hearted expression when asking for a blessing from a god or from an older person.

Prasad(am)—*Prasad(am)* is food, sweets, *kumkum* or ashes, or flowers—first offered to god, and then considered blessed—that are then given to people as symbolic aspects of a blessing. People will bring some home from visits to temples and give it to their friends and families as a gesture of affection, inclusion in their prayers, and a religious blessing.

The literal meaning of *Prasad* is "gracious gift." An intentional offering is made to God, asking for blessing, and then the blessed object is given to others.

A traditional family may put clothes for a specific purpose before the altar or gods in the *puja* room, say a prayer, and only then use the new clothes. More commonly, food is offered first to God and only then consumed or distributed. In some families, dessert is offered to the gods on Fridays and then everyone in the family gets a little piece of it. In other families, the most basic of foods cooked everyday—for example, rice——is offered first to God, a small spoon of it is taken out and set in the *puja* room, and the rest is consumed. It could be understood as a different form of grace before a meal, or a conversion of material to spiritual form.

Puja—*Puja*, pronounced "pooh ja," means worship, prayer, or rituals connected with either. A puja room is a place designated for worship and reflection. It could be a room in the home, a shelf, a cupboard, or other physical space dedicated to gods and goddesses, idols of favorite gods or goddesses, often including a space for incense and lamps. *Pujas* are done daily, occasionally, on or for specific purposes (*e.g.*, a baby's birth, moving into a new house, or a death ritual) and can be either informal or formal. It is a term from Sanskrit and is mainly used in Hinduism, but can also be used for Buddhist, Jain, or Sikh worship.

Rama—See the **Ramayana**

Ramayana, The—In another great epic, *The Ramayana*, god Rama, an incarnation of Vishnu, is the dutiful crown prince who leaves his rightful kingdom for exile in the forests of India accompanied by his faithful wife *Seetha* and his brother *Lakshmana*. *Rama's* father, the aging king, grants one of his three wives a boon when she saves his life. She asks that *Rama*, the crown prince and his son by another of his wives, be sent away for fourteen years so that her son may become king. *Rama* leaves the kingdom, upholding his father's honor but also breaking his heart. His brother *Bharata* defies his mother and rules in *Rama's* name, placing *Rama's* wooden shoes on the throne. *Rama's* wife *Seetha* is kidnapped by the evil king of Sri Lanka, and a monkey king helps *Rama* find and rescue her.

The Ramayana is full of tales of valor, devotion, and bravery. *Rama* is also an incarnation of god *Vishnu*, but does not perform miracles and supernatural feats. He is a mortal and shows mortal failings and weaknesses, and thus is a more easily accessible hero.

Samsara—The cycle of material life including life and death. It also refers to the cyclicity of life, death and rebirth.

Saraswati—The consort of Vishnu, *Saraswati* is the goddess of learning, music, and wisdom.

Seetha—See **Deepavali or Diwali**; also see **The Ramayana**

Shiva—*Shiva* is the god of destruction who keeps the balance in the world, maintaining the cycle of birth and death. His cosmic dance has components of *lasya*, or grace, and *tandava*, or power. He is depicted as ashen-skinned, clad in tiger skins, wearing snakes around his neck, hair piled high and in it is the goddess *Ganges* (who comes to earth from his head so that she does not destroy the earth with her power). He also has a blue neck where *Parvati* traps poisons churned up from the oceans, a crescent moon in his hair, a trident as his weapon, a third eye which, when opened, could destroy the world; and he carries a drum depicting transcendence. He is widely worshiped in the form of a phallic symbol and as the god of yoga, meditation, and art. He also has a peaceful aspect when he is worshipped as a yogi who is in deep meditation and who is the father figure of *Ganesha* and *Murugan*. His vehicle is a bull, and most temples to *Shiva* have a statue of a bull facing the main deity. See also **Parvati**.

Shudras—The lowermost strata in the caste system, who do menial work. Later they came to be known as *Dalits* or *Harijans*.

Solpa Adjust Maadee—*Solpa* means "just a bit," "adjust" is obvious, and *maadee* means "make or do." The phrase is often supplemented with a honorific like *swami* [sir], preceded by *deyvittu* [in god's name], or with a physical gesture like putting all the right hand finger tips together or the right hand palm turned up at a 45-degree angle. It is used to make a request of another person when a favor is being asked.

Svarga—Heavenly place.
See also **Naraka and Svarga.**

Talaq, Talaq, Talaq—The Muslim community in India is more than 170 million people strong. The laws of the country allow them to have a separate family law as they were considered a minority deserving special latitude at the time of Partition. The "triple *Talaq*" law allows a Muslim man to say the words in person, correspondence, or over an Internet connection—over a period of time or in the same sentence and time—and thereby legally divorce his wife. She did not need to be present. The same privilege was not offered to women. Children from the marriage came under guardianship of the father.

Another religious law allows the Muslim man to decide on the support payments to his ex-wife. The woman can appeal to a religious board for a change in the support payments, not to a civil legal entity. Similarly, the *Sharia* law allows a Muslim girl to be married after age 15 (and not 18 as accorded by civil law), and also sanctions polygamy.

The triple *Talaq* is a controversial law and, at this time in 2017, the Supreme Court in India has finally deemed it unconstitutional. The *Bharatiya Janata* Party is now trying to enforce a uniform civil code for all people irrespective of religion.

Tandava—Powerful dance of god Shiva. See *Lasya* above.

Vaishyas—In the caste system, third stratum beneath the *Brahmins* and the *Kshatriyas*. These are the traders.

Vegetarianism—A good majority of the population of India is vegetarian. Most vegetarians in India do not eat eggs but do consume dairy products. The basis of vegetarianism is *ahimsa* or non-violence. The focus is on not destroying life, even incipient life. Most people in India say "veg" for vegetarian and non-veg or "NV" for meat-eating.

Vegetarians consider non-vegetarian food to be polluting of a calm and peaceful lifestyle, and also polluting because of death and germs. They may also consider that lower-caste people were part of the process of butchering the meat; and that would be another reason to avoid such foods or even kitchens where meat is cooked. In many homes where meat is also cooked, there are rules of purity and pollution that keep foods in separate areas and vessels. In most eating establishments, there is a general awareness and courtesy that vegetarian sensibilities need to be protected. Some people give up meat-eating as they get older so that they can cultivate more habits of calmness and serenity and this earns them respect in the community.

It is understood that castes and communities that produce soldiers and those that do hard physical labor need to eat meat. It once was the case that the upper castes of Brahmins, who were priests and teachers, did not eat meat. Even if Hindus eat meat, they avoid beef, as the cow is considered sacred.

Vishnu **and** *Lakshmi*—*Vishnu* is the preserver of the world. He is the preserver/ protector who comes to earth as an Avatar when the world is threatened by evil or chaos. He is usually depicted with four arms and has a lotus, a conch, a spinning discus, and a mace.

His counterpart is the goddess *Lakshmi,* who is the giver of wealth and prosperity, both material and spiritual. They are sometimes depicted together on the unending serpent in a dreamy state, imagining the world into being. *Vishnu* is depicted as ever present in everything and is said to have ten incarnations or Avatars. *Lakshmi* has several names, too, in her many incarnations as the consort of *Vishnu*—*Sita* as *Rama's* wife and *Rukmini* as one of *Krishna's* wives.

In some interpretations, Jesus Christ and Buddha are also *Vishnu's* avatars. Thus Hinduism easily absorbs other religious symbolism. He is expected anytime now as the *Kalki* avatar (with a flaming sword on a white horse) to end this current epoch.

Yama—Another name for *Dharma*, the God of Death. *Yudhishtira*, the god of life and duty and death, was the son of Yama, and was the Pandava king who led a virtuous life.

Yogas—The yogas are pathways to a richer and more harmonious way of life leading to *Moksha*. Yoga can be practiced through exercise and calm reflection, devotion, through study, or even by means of charitable works and helping others.

Yudhisthtira—The firstborn and eldest brother of the warrior *Arjuna*. He was the son of *Dharma* (or *Yama*, the God of Death), known for his adherence to truth and rightful living. He leads the Pandavas to victory after the Mahabharata war.

Artistic depiction of Bhagawad Gita where Krishna
is teaching Arjuna about Dharma

Popular Calendar art – Shiva, Parvati, Murugan and Ganesha

South Indian temple representation of Ganesha with his mother Parvati seated on his leg as he rides his mouse

Popular calendar art – Vishnu with his consorts Bhu (earth) Devi and Sri (spiritual) Devi astride his bird-like mount Garuda

Brahma the 4 headed creator on his swan in a North Indian artistic representation

*South Indian artistic vision of Saraswathi
the goddess of music, language and learning*

God Vishnu (as represented in a Pahari miniature painting) relaxing on the serpent of Time AnantaSesha with his consort Laksmi the goddess of wealth. Out of his navel arises the lotus of life on which sits Brahma.

Two young girls lighting lamps for Diwali

Special Diwali offerings of foods and fruits to the Gods in a home puja room in South India

Shiva as Nataraja or the God of Dance and Theatre. He is represented here as a bronze statue dancing the rhythm of life and cosmic truth, holding a rattle drum in one hand (death and primeval reverberations), a fire in another hand that burns and destroys but also illuminates and energizes, a third hand bestows blessing, and his fourth hand points downwards in a gesture of an elephant's trunk, removing obstacles. One leg is lifted in a gesture of promise of eternal bliss to the devoted. Around him is the great wheel of Samsara the endless circle of births, deaths and rebirths while he tramples the demon of ignorance,

CPSIA information can be obtained
at www.ICGtesting.com
Printed in the USA
LVOW05s0003050318
568641LV00008B/505/P